HONEYMOON ROUND THE WORLD

Dominique and Aliette Lapierre are a young French couple who, at the age of twenty, chose to spend their honeymoon travelling round the world earning the costs of their journey as they went along. Starting in New York, they drove across to San Francisco, calling in on Mexico on the way, where they earned their passages to Japan; from Japan to Korea, and then by boat to Hong Kong, Siam, and India, then across India by train to Pakistan and through Afghanistan, Kabul, and Persia to Palestine and then home to Paris. Here is a gay account of the world as seen through the eyes of a young French couple, described with complete sincerity and truth.

Dominique
Lapierre

Honeymoon
Round the World

Preface by
André Maurois

Translated by
Helen Beauclerk

London
Secker & Warburg
1957

This book is dedicated to the
Two Thérésitas

And to the friends I have met on the
world's highways.

Printed in England by
Western Printing Services Ltd, Bristol
and
first published 1957
by
Martin Secker & Warburg Ltd
7 John Street, London
WC1

Contents

		Page
	Preface by André Maurois	9
1.	New York: Marriage	15
2.	Virginia: The Seventh Wonder of the World	18
3.	Mexico: The Hunt for Pesos	20
4.	On the Shores of the Pacific with Robinson Crusoe	25
5.	Sharks by Night	29
6.	A Village Festival	31
7.	An Old French Priest ends his Life in the Sierra	33
8.	Arizona and the Best Sandwiches in the Desert	35
9.	Hollywood: Forty Dollars easily earned	40
10.	San Francisco: We become Salesmen in a Big Store	44
11.	Cocktails at Honolulu	56
12.	Yokohama and only Nineteen Dollars Left	60
13.	Our First Evening in Japan	63
14.	First Impressions	67
15.	How Aliette became a Professor	70
16.	Touring the Land of the Rising Sun	72
17.	Hiroshima and the Largest Cathedral in the World	75
18.	A Visit to the Marionettes	80
19.	Mikimoto's Fabulous Isle	82
20.	Off to Korea	85
21.	A Front-line Feast	89
22.	Touring Korea with Marshal Juin	97
23.	Aliette as a Professor	101
24.	The Sufferings of the Young in Korea	109

25. Aliette's Triumph   117
26. An Excursion into China   119
27. Looking for Gambling-hells in Macao   124
28. En Route for the Venice of the East   128
29. Round and About the Menam   132
30. Aliette wants to smoke Opium   135
31. The First Nightmares of Our Honeymoon   138
32. First Encounters: These People frighten us   144
33. In Darkest India   150
34. The Lepers of Benares   158
35. Hunting the Man-eater   164
36. A Difficult Journey to Pakistan   176
37. Through Afghanistan   187
38. Lost in the Desert   192
39. At Teheran   202
40. End of the Honeymoon Round the World   210

List of Illustrations

facing page

1. In Guadalajara   32
2. The market in Zacatlan   32
3. A village church in Mexico   33
4. Japanese street-singers   48
5. Japanese fire-brigade   48
6. The authors in Japan   49
7. Japanese potter   49
8. Korean children near Seoul   96
9. The food queue, Korea   96
10. On the borders of Communist China   97
11. Houses in the New Territories, Hong Kong   97
12. Temple statue, Bangkok   112
13. Temple sculpture, Bubaneshwar, India   112
14. Siamese children at play   113
15. Indian beggar   113
16. Taxi-rank, Bubaneshwar   160
17. Street scene, Benares   160
18. Bathing in the Ganges, Benares   161
19. A visit to a *souk*   161
20. Goldsmiths at work, Afghanistan   176
21. An Afghan villager   176
22. Mosque at Ispahan   177
23. A village street, Zahidan   177

Preface

THERE are intellectual fashions. For some years now black has been the mental wear. French writers are fond of saying that France is in a state of moral decline, that the young people have lost courage. Such generalities are untrue, as are most generalities. France is not as sick as our lucid pessimists make out, and there is no lack of brave young Frenchmen. If proof were needed, a boy and a girl, husband and wife, supply it.

Dominique and Aliette Lapierre are a very young couple who chose to spend their honeymoon, their wedding trip, going round the world. The world, nothing less, at twenty. . . . The husband had trained himself by travelling at seventeen, without money, through Mexico and the United States; after which he attended the Paris *École des Sciences Politiques*, won a Fullbright Scholarship, and spent some time at Lafayette College in Pennsylvania.

His wife, Aliette, had worked on the *Jardin des Modes* in Paris and then, wishing to study American methods, on the New York staff of *Harper's Bazaar*. They met, they liked each other, they were married at the New York City Hall. Their witnesses were the president of Twentieth Century Fox, the son of a well-known Italian singer, and a lady novelist from the Far West. A very American marriage for a very French pair.

Whereupon they set out on their grand tour. Cash in hand: 300 dollars. The Lapierres are not of those sturdy beggars who walk the earth today, insisting, nobody knows why, as though it were their due, upon board and lodging and whatnot, free. They wanted to come back to France by the Pacific Ocean and Asia "to see what was going on in the world", they said. But they were determined to pay their way as they went.

How they did so is told in this book. It is all a miracle, constantly renewed; but is not every life a series of miracles? As soon as funds threatened to fall below danger-point, they stopped and filled up the tank. In San Francisco they each found work at one of that city's two largest stores. In Japan it was Aliette who, in masterly fashion, replenished the family funds by designing a collection of dresses, thereby earning, in one month, enough to pay for the return journey.

A wonderful start in life. It can but confer a basic self-confidence and the certainty that, come what may, in no matter what part of the world you may be, you will find a way out. In our present ever-changing society, no one can foresee the future. The great thing is to know that we are able to face any and every event and deal with it. There is nothing like a journey such as this, boldly and happily undertaken, to form such steady, reliant natures.

This is not, to young people, the only advantage of getting to know lands unknown before. At a time when humanity must understand that it is a question of uniting or perishing; when all problems are linked; when some act of injustice committed in Korea, or Iran, may lead to war in Europe; when lack of understanding between peoples makes the task of government impossible owing to the popular resentment at any compromise or conciliation—this is the time when the best brains should have true, world-wide experience.

Admittedly such knowledge cannot be acquired by study alone. "A prince does not learn his duty from a book." The published work, however excellent, about a country the reader has never seen does not provide sufficient information. Almost invariably the author has his prejudices. Above all, our attention is not easily caught by an image that wakens no memory, no emotion; whereas, so long as we have *seen* even cursorily, any new information will be interesting and will take its place among the network of our own ideas.

I am a case in point. For the greater part of my life I found it impossible to be more than mildly interested in Latin America. I felt I was wrong but could do nothing about it. In 1947 I went for a long journey and stayed for a considerable time in those parts. Since then everything that happens there makes sense to me. I understand the local problems; I have friends there; I can guess at their reactions. Two months' acquaintance did more than six years' study.

Because they have travelled through the United States, because they have encountered the kindliness and generosity that make the Americans so charming, because they have admired and acquired the qualities of hard work and good organisation that form the greatness of that country, the Lapierres will never be counted amongst those Frenchmen who can be persuaded that America either lacks any civilisation, or possesses one totally different from our own. The Lapierres are and will always be completely French. French in appearance, in tastes, in intelligence. But they will never lose touch with America; they will do all they can to make the Americans know what is best in us and to learn in return what is best in them.

It is this new breadth of mind and spirit that is the essential gift of their fantastic tour. The Englishman, Charles Lamb, having begun a sentence with the words: "I hate that man . . ." was interrupted.

"But, Mr Lamb, you don't know him!"

"Naturally," retorted Lamb. "Do you think I could be so wicked as to hate a man I knew?"

Maybe one cannot avoid detesting detestable people, but the most dangerous are the collective hatreds, the hatreds of a whole people for another people they do not know.

In countries where you do not speak the language, a quick survey is not enough to understand minds wholly different from your own. The Lapierres found Asia mysterious, secret, veiled in a politeness that did not imply agreement. They admired Japan, her vitality, her arts, her taste; they did not feel that they had got behind the mask. In fact they did not do so. And that is even more true of India and Pakistan.

Yet even there actual contact was not wasted. To realise that Asia presents Europe with problems that are far from being solved, is, at least, to have acquired a new and valuable modesty. We—ourselves and our allies—have all too many augurs and experts interpreting for us, with the utmost assurance, the will of this or that Asiatic group. We need wise and patient men who by prolonged and intimate acquaintance can break through the shell of politeness to the true thoughts within. Were such men to be found, were they to write of their discoveries, then the Lapierres of this world would read their books with intelligence and curiosity, for to them Korea, Afghanistan, Macao would evoke clear and precise images. Images are the natural supports of ideas.

The difference between Dominique Lapierre's memories and those of older travellers is very remarkable. Past generations sought either to be dramatic (Alexander Dumas père) or to evolve some doctrine, some set of principles (Alexis de Tocqueville) from their experiences. This young man of our own day has no concern for literary effects or for doctrinaire conclusions. He tells us what he saw, what he did, with absolute simplicity. To every country he comes without preconceived notions. He does not analyse his feelings. He is altogether objective.

And he and his like are clever with their hands. Alone in the desert, Dominique managed to get his car out of a serious breakdown. Aliette was able to improvise, in a few days, with Japanese materials and without competent assistance, a collection of Haute Couture models. "Think with your hands," was Denis de Rougemont's advice. The mind has its share, but work brings us constantly down to earth. Which is as it should be. Deprived of contact with reality, thought can but vainly beat its wings in the void.

ADVICE TO YOUNG FRENCH PEOPLE WHO WISH TO TRAVEL ROUND THE WORLD

First, travel round France. To understand the unknown you must begin with the known.

Make sure before you start that you can earn your living as you go. For this two things are necessary: to speak one or more languages besides French; to have a thorough knowledge of one technique. The man who gets help is the man who can make himself useful.

Do not judge. We seem as bizarre and absurd to foreigners as they seem to us.

Do not censure; try to understand and love.

In the least friendly land there will always be friends for those who deserve them.

Learn, in the East, to change your standard of values. A Japanese begins by saying "Yes", because he has no word for "No". At your first meeting you imagine he is making an assertion. Not at all; he is questioning you: "Is it not true that? . . ." He will make up his mind slowly, but his decision, once taken, can be trusted. Actually he has a high sense of honour. But don't ask him to adopt your instincts in place of his own.

The Oriental can read, on your face, your every thought; you can read nothing from his.

In America the password is: Frankness and Good Will.

The Englishman is a mixture of West and East. Here too politeness is a wall and instinct is stronger than reason. The American expects you to give him explanations; the Englishman wants a statement.

Wherever you go, defend your own country, do not attack the other man's. You cannot condemn a whole people.

A home-loving Frenchman (Raymond Poincaré) once said: "As soon as you leave the place de la Concorde, reason vanishes." That is not true. On the contrary, reason vanishes if you never leave the place de la Concorde. But you must come back to it from time to time. Antaeus regained his strength by touching his Mother Earth.

And now away with you! have no thought or ambition save of reaching your next stage. Like Saul seeking his father's asses, you will discover a kingdom. But the kingdom will be within you.

ANDRÉ MAUROIS,
of the Académie Française

1

New York: Marriage

IT WAS hot and oppressive the day I got married; the least effort made me sweat.

I took our two witnesses to fetch Aliette in a long red taxi. One of them, Damiato, son of a well-known Italian tenor and my host for the past month, kept on running the tip of his tongue over his black moustache and sleeking back his glossy hair with quick strokes of his pocket-comb. He chain-smoked Camel after Camel, talking in a low voice with his head turned towards Saint-Léger, erstwhile manager of the Metropolitan Opera House and now vice-president of Twentieth Century Fox, who had settled back comfortably, with a benign smile, against the padded red leather cushions.

We picked up Aliette, looking very elegant in her white summer frock.

We went along the East River and, once we were down-town, cut across New York from east to west till we came to a stop before a building that stretched out in every direction: the New York City Hall. In front of the colossal entrance porch we collected our third witness, the great American novelist Gladys Shaw Erskine, ex-cowgirl from the Far West. Her sixty or so years were indiscernible beneath the leaves and flowers of her hat and an aggressive thickness of pink face-powder. Her faithful and devoted "Major", an ex-Indian Army officer, was twiddling his polished cane as he marked time beside her.

Together we climbed the steps of the staircase leading, so a huge gold-lettered notice-board informed us, to the Marriage Hall. Gladys gave a sharp push to a frosted-glass door, and there we were in a vast room, criss-crossed by long tables and benches, that gave it the appearance of a waiting-room in a police station. At

15

the far end were ranged a number of pay-desks behind which, protected by a grille, several clerks with rolled-up shirt-sleeves were stamping goodness knows what documents.

We sat down. Sprawled across a near-by table, an enormous young negress was chatting away to her husband-to-be, a pale-faced skimpy half-breed who astonished us at regular intervals by letting out a bellow of coarse laughter.

"Lapierre!" shouted a small man in rimless glasses.

All our group moved over to the left, where the witnesses signed their names, quite illegibly, in an imposing book. A short pause and we found ourselves in a small room like a Protestant chapel furnished with church candles on a makeshift altar. A door burst open and the official uniter stepped briskly in. He took hold of my hand and Aliette's, at the same time smiling in a manner that accentuated the slit of his hare-lip. He drew us towards a tubular neon light, and, turning round with his back to it, he began in a slow unctuous tone:

"Dominique, do you take this woman to be . . . ?

"And you, Aliette . . . ?"

The end of each word trailed off into an endless tremolo. He kept his very blue gaze fixed upon us and from time to time wriggled his neck in his impeccable, white stand-up collar.

We lunched with Gladys, who lived in Greenwich Village, New York's Montparnasse. Her odd little doll's house was set in the courtyard of an immense block of flats; one had to duck one's head on entering, and the elephant bells, brought back by the Major from one of his campaigns, started to jingle inside the door. On one wall was a large photograph of Gladys clasped to the bosom of Buffalo Bill. A heavy scent arose from an incense-burner.

After a delicious light Californian claret, the Major was in great form and took us for a trip round Manhattan on a pleasure-steamer.

"On your left, ladies and gentlemen," shouts the guide through his loudspeaker, "you see the tallest building in the world. On your right you have the Maxwell House factory, the biggest coffee factory in the world. We are now passing the impressive S.S. *United States*, the fastest liner in the world. . . ."

Beside me a small boy piped up: "But, Pop, it sure ain't the biggest in the world?" "No," his father answered, "but that don't matter. The *Queen Elizabeth* is the biggest but she can't pass through the Panama Canal."

". . . Now, ladies and gentlemen, we are facing the gigantic telephone exchange where more than three million calls are put through every minute . . ."

The *Flandre*, on her maiden voyage, was given no more than a parenthetical word or two from our guide. It should be said that the poor thing was being towed in by the harbour tugs; her engines were out of order and there was not sufficient power left in her batteries to allow her sirens to answer the blasts of greeting discharged by all the other ships' hooters—a positively appalling hullabaloo.

". . . And now we see before us the sensational apartment-houses that de-mon-strate the mag-ni-fi-cent social policy of our beloved mayor. These apartments cost only fifty dollars a month. To qualify for one of them you must earn less than seventy-five dollars a week and have more than two children under fifteen years of age . . ."

The rest of the afternoon was spent in a whirl of figures and statistics. What if the guide who takes foreign visitors round Notre-Dame were to say: "Ladies and gentlemen, the construction of this cathedral took 5,000 tons of stone and 2,000 square feet of stained glass. The labourers' wage per hour was . . ."

B

2

Virginia: The Seventh Wonder of the World

NEXT day, aboard an antique Dodge purchased for thirty dollars, we left New York in a thin drizzle under leaden skies. Our luggage was lashed into the "spider" with old pieces of string and rusty wire. I could see it at times in the driving mirror, swaying perilously.

Our entire fortune amounted to 300 dollars. With this modest sum we proposed going round the world for our honeymoon. Neither of us realised for a moment the folly of such an undertaking. Very soon, the daily or rather the twice-daily problems of filling up the car with petrol and ourselves with sandwiches (for several weeks we ate nothing else), and that of finding a bed for the night, nearly shattered our illusions and forced us to abandon our project.

We had no knapsacks, no special equipment, for we both detest "camping". Aliette had packed more evening dresses than shorts into her innumerable bags and valises that squashed us in between the badly fitting doors.

On the splendid highways of New Jersey and Pennsylvania, we spent the first hours of a round trip that was to take many months and give rise to adventures at almost every turn of our sixty-thousand-mile venture.

We arrived one morning in Virginia. The road was lined with huge hoardings advertising a "Spectacle unique in all the world", "A natural bridge with the river flowing beneath and the highway above". In addition the posters proclaimed, "George Washington carved his initials on this rock". The whole thing, methodically and in all seriousness, had been dubbed "The Seventh Wonder of the World". The temptation was too great and we pulled up. Below us, in the space round a big hotel, hundreds of cars were packed, their bumpers richly festooned with multicoloured streamers displaying in letters of gold, "Come and see the Seventh . . ." Inside the hotel, a large lounge, ablaze with neon lights, dazzled us with its "drugstores", souvenir kiosks, pictures, luscious pink postcards, photomatons, cigarette machines, tele-phone booths, and deafened us with the staccato music blaring forth from loudspeakers set in the ceiling. On all sides were numberless pay-desks to relieve the traveller of the ritual dollar, as readily dispensed with in America as are a hundred francs in France.

A little path led down to a stream of thick muddy water and on to the entrance of a sort of grotto, above which, enticed by the debauch of advertisements, several touring-cars were already slowing down. We walked on by the river, all agog for the Seventh Wonder. A peremptory whistle called us back, just as the same staccato music suddenly burst forth under the stone vault. All we could see was a rocky surface with hundreds of scored initials, among which Aliette had great fun in discovering seventy-one G. S.'s. And that was that.

We emerged greatly disappointed and resolved never to look for the remaining six "wonders". We did not know then that our wanderings over the face of the globe would provide us with plenty of others, and those far more genuine.

3

Mexico: The Hunt for Pesos

WE DROVE on by easy stages to the Mexican frontier, where at once everything became different. We stopped at a roadside café, high in the mountains, to refresh ourselves. At the next table a superb beggar, with large dark eyes and a resplendent grizzled beard, lay slumped on a decrepit chair with a cup of coffee in front of him; his stick and meagre bundle were beside him on the dried-mud floor. He glanced up at us and his long tapering fingers reached out for his cup of coffee. We could not resist the chance of a photograph. He was delighted, and we offered him beer and sandwiches. I was just preparing my camera and flash when there was a sudden eruption in the room and a puny, scrubby little man, who had already taken a dislike to me, after administering a kick to the beggar, shook me by the waist as he shouted in Spanish:

"Filthy foreigner! Filthy American! You've come to spy on us! You want to see our wretched state! You want to show your photographs and bring shame on us and tell everyone how miserable we are. Dirty *gringo!*"

He turned back to the beggar, who was slowly rising to his feet, gave him another push and threw him out of the café.

"I am a Frenchman," I explained. "I have not the slightest intention of decrying Mexico or the Mexicans."

The little man quietened down; he ceased frothing at the mouth and the fury went out of his voice. He drew up a chair, called to the waiter, ordered several bottles of beer, and the scene ended most amicably with his seeing us off and wishing us Godspeed in the warmest manner. When we later passed the beggar in a cloud of dust, he waved a nonchalant hand.

We were to find a similar inferiority complex, often amounting to xenophobia, in India and Pakistan, in Iran and the Far East.

A great sprawl of light shining in the darkness: Mexico City. Uprooted trees and deep, water-filled ruts—positive rivers—made the approaches difficult. For the past three weeks it had been deluging with rain. The result was almost catastrophic. Mexico City, built on a dried-up lake, is slowly but steadily sinking. The massive Opera House will soon vanish into a hole; its statues have been removed long ago to lighten the weight.

The mains had burst and the sewers had split the asphalt and were flooding the streets; in certain parts of the town you could only get about in boats. Many of the houses were subsiding unevenly, cracking and threatening to crumble to pieces; here and there, to prevent the final collapse, they had been shored up; everywhere cement was being poured into the weakened foundations. The papers spoke of millions of dollars lost and the need to rebuild the whole city!

We found lodgings with an elderly Spanish lady, who owned a charming villa not far from the smart Lomas quarter. After a long refreshing bath we took stock of our position. What stood out a mile was that we were remarkably short of money, and that we must earn some at once. In Mexico, lectures and newspaper articles are always a good line; Aliette gave a talk on Fashion on the radio and I on Travel at the *Alliance Française*. The pesos came in very handy to pay doctor's and chemist's bills, for I went down with fever—typhoid they called it—and spent ten days in bed with a temperature of a hundred and four.

After that a spell of convalescence seemed desirable and a change of air, so we plumped for the Pacific coast. Somewhere near Manzanillo Luis Bunuel was filming his *Robinson Crusoe*. Unfortunately my illness had left us completely broke and we could not start until we had found some more pesos. Unfortunately, too, the Mexican papers—like most papers the world over —pay badly and what you earn is hardly worth the interminable hours you spend waiting for an interview. Especially in that land of *mañana*. The only Mexican paper that paid decent rates was *Voz*, the official Government organ, run by the President's seventeen-year-old son. I decided to pay a call on this young man. His offices were in the National Lottery skyscraper in the centre of the city. The lifts, of course, were not working and I had to climb the seventeen storeys on foot.

At length I reached a huge office decorated in pale green. Below its great bay windows the whole town lay spread and in the distance towered Popocatepetl, white in its eternal snows.

A rather over-made-up secretary greeted me and asked me my business.

"I have come to call on Miguel Aleman junior."

"Miguelito?"

I suffered a momentary shock in hearing a mere secretary call the son of the President of the Republic, the director of an important publication, by his pet name.

"Miguelito is out. He is opening an electric power station in the Chiapas. Can you come back on Tuesday?"

I went back on Tuesday at the time appointed. The fine green leather arm-chairs of the waiting-room were occupied by distinguished-looking old gentlemen in stiff collars and patent leather shoes.

I waited a good hour, but no Miguelito. Finally, losing my patience, I appealed to the secretary, who twiddled the knobs of her telephone, chattered into it and presently produced another young lady who was very sorry for El Señor Lapierre . . . "but Miguelito is terribly busy and can't see you till tomorrow."

Next day, after another hour among the old gentlemen, I lost my temper. "I will not leave this place till I have seen your chief. I have come a great distance and expect to be treated courteously."

The secretary gave me a seductive smile and led me into another big room closely guarded by commissionaires. A gentleman of about forty, wearing a black tie, rose and welcomed me in French. I strode boldly forward.

"*Buenos días, Señor Director.*"

"I am not the director, only the editor. . . ."

Another long wait with only the photographs pinned on the walls to distract me. Finally a bell rang; a curly-haired commissionaire took me into a still larger room, whose doors were handsomely upholstered in leather. This time it was surely the boss himself who came towards me and crushed my hand in his plump, hairy paw! But once again no! "Miguelito will see you in a moment." I became more and more impatient. Was I never to set eyes on the Great Man? I fiddled with the pages of my manuscript.

But this time not for long. The lovely secretary took me by the arm, gave her hips an alluring wriggle and conducted me via an inner staircase to a small office on the next flight. The walls were entirely covered with photographs; there was a tiger skin upon the floor. I was in the presence of a boy who couldn't possibly be more than eighteen, the President of Mexico's son, the director of *Voz*. His wavy black hair was brushed smoothly back; a many-coloured silk scarf, held by a gold pin, encircled his neck; he was wearing black cowboy boots. On the mantelshelf was a large picture of Rita Hayworth inscribed: "To Miguel, with love from Rita." Near by, Truman's portrait jostled Auriol's; behind the super-editorial desk was a huge photograph of a negress, naked in her native jungle. She was reading *Voz*.

And everywhere Miguel: Miguel on an elephant, Miguel with dead lions at his feet; Miguel gazing at a giraffe or a zebra. Shining through the glass top of his writing-table was a star-burst of pretty women in bathing dresses.

I showed him my piece. Everything was settled within three minutes, and he started to tell me of his big-game hunting in Africa. The telephone rang. He lifted the receiver with a casual air. There was some talk of Chicago. An accountant appeared and paid me for my manuscript in cash. I thanked my adolescent patron and left him to his more important affairs.

For the past week a unanimous press had been praising his father and his father's great works. Señor Aleman's term of office was coming to an end and you could not open a paper without being confronted with banner headlines: "The National Oil Company of Mexico congratulates the Señor Presidente on his magnificent accomplishment and offers its heartfelt wishes." "The Port of Vera Cruz gives thanks to the greatest of all Mexican Presidents for his prodigious activity." The cathedral of Mexico City was covered with banners saluting "Aleman, Mexico's greatest hero". He was showered with confetti wherever he went, and school children walked daily in procession to lay a bouquet of flowers, in his name, at the feet of the Angel of Independence. He spent the last days of his seven-year reign in inaugurating hospitals, railroads, factories, etc., even where the buildings themselves were still unfinished. His daughter was about to be married. Her presents included over forty Cadillacs, seventy-five TV sets and dozens of washing-machines.

Mexico is a land of violent contrasts; nowhere did we meet with such opulence and such poverty. An aggressive and highly sensitive national pride demands a God, and Aleman, supported by his ministers and a vigorous publicity campaign uplifted by his candidature for the Nobel Peace Prize, had taken on the part. The illiterate peasants know nothing of him but his name, despite his seven years of office.

Yet there is no doubt that what he has done is important, even though it has cost the country ten times more than it should have done. Everyone knows that the régime has created many tidy fortunes, but there is always the consolation of remembering that Mexico's former administrators were infinitely worse.

4

On the Shores of the Pacific with Robinson Crusoe

WITH Miguelito's pesos we made a dash for the Saint-Lazare railway station to take the first train for Manzanillo, the little seaport on the Pacific.

The train was an express, due to start at 20.01 hours, and we waited comfortably enough in our carriages for the appointed time. At 20.45 hours the train had not yet left the station. To put our minds at rest, we stepped out on to the platform to inquire the cause of the delay. A group of men were busied over the steam-pipes between two coaches, which were apparently disconnected. Though we knew Mexico to be a highly specialised country, we were much impressed to see that four workmen were required for the job: one, armed with a pair of huge pincers, to unscrew the nuts, a second to remove the bolts, a third to take off the washers, a fourth to replace the worn parts. The operation was then repeated in reverse.

Mexican sleeping-cars are similar to those of the United States; they have a long corridor lined on either side with recesses, as in a catacomb. The passengers are not always over-clean in their habits, and it is quite a common thing in the middle of the night to have the skin of a peeled orange bang in your face from the bunk overhead.

Mexico holds the world record for railway accidents, but they seldom amount to catastrophes, the average speed of the trains being extremely slow. Delays are a "regular occurrence" for the simple reason that the company pays generous overtime and it is therefore in the drivers' best interest to drive their powerful American engines as slowly as possible.

We made the acquaintance of our particular drivers at one of the many little palm-girt stations where our train was scheduled to call. Along the platform, the whole length of our five coaches, were arrayed benches and trestle-tables. Tortillas, rolls flavoured with cinnamon and covered with flies, sweets thick with wasps, coconuts and salads and bowls of curd were spread in profusion, and every traveller sat down to them for an indeterminate period of time. The greediest were our two engine-drivers. Nothing would induce them to go back to their cabs till they had partaken of a copious and repulsive meal. The less voracious of the two owned a guitar and started to thrum on it as soon as he had finished eating. His mate promptly fell to with redoubled energy and the meal ended in great gales of laughter and the nostalgic melody of one of the marvellous Mexican songs.

Despite all this we arrived only a few hours late at Manzanillo. It was not so very far from the strip of jungle and beach where Bunuel was shooting his *Crusoe*.

As we got out of the train the first person I ran into, much to my surprise, was my old friend D . . . . , the stout headmaster of Mexico City's French lycée, whose even stouter wife sold sweet-meats in the school playground at ten every morning. It was said she carried the art of trading so far as to present every boy who bought three oranges with a piece of elastic so that he could make a catapult and use the skins as missiles. D . . . . came originally from Béziers; he greeted me with true Southern kindliness unimpaired by twenty years of Mexico. He suggested introducing us to Bunuel straight away, a proposal that filled us with joy.

We found a stocky little man, his head protected by a faded topee, his back wrapped in a bath-towel, trotting about in the rocks that overhang the Pacific Ocean. "Meet Luis Bunuel, the cruellest producer in the world!" He wiped his forehead on the back of his arm and shouted in Spanish: "Hi! Boys! Over here!"

A gang of Indians, naked to the waist and flourishing machetes, arived shouting on the scene and quickly cleared the required space. A lanky, fair-haired fellow, bent double under his heavy load, brought up the camera and set it in position. Two other assistants followed with the accumulators. The bay is lined with huge coconut-trees, and as far as the eye could see huge green rollers came crashing in along the empty sands. They were preparing to shoot the wreck of Crusoe's raft.

Bunuel sat down on a shaky camp-stool, puffing nervously at his Lucky Strikes, one finger pressed to the drum of his right ear, in which he is almost deaf. His face was drenched with sweat; his attention was everywhere at once, and he rapped out his orders in a deep, staccato voice. A speck in the distance, Crusoe's raft could be seen approaching, vanishing every moment in the trough of the waves. Bunuel turned to us and laughed:

"The real Crusoe isn't on the raft. We're using a stand-in. . . . One has come to think from the book that Crusoe is a sort of Tarzan. Mine will be the complete opposite. He can't swim, he is afraid to walk barefoot because of the ants. When he sees some small insect on a tree he shrieks out, 'A scorpion!' "

He suddenly leapt to his feet, shouting "Alex! Alex!" and hurried towards the camera-man, a lazy-looking, untidily dressed person wearing a knotted handkerchief for collar and a belt so weighted with gauges and recorders and instruments of all sorts that it scarcely kept his trousers up. Bunuel stood on the top of the rock, one hand on the camera and the other, megaphone-wise, to his mouth. "Action!" he yelled. Fifty yards below, a huge wave overturned the raft and the substitute Crusoe.

That evening, after a long day's work in the broiling sun, we found Bunuel alone at his hotel. The season was over and the place almost empty. He was seated in a cane chair beside a bottle of gin and an ice-box. Every now and then he picked up a crumpled piece of paper, scribbled a few lines on it in his tiny handwriting, lit another cigarette from the butt of the last one, throwing away the butt, and stared out to the sea which he hated. He had been there for ten weeks waiting to film a storm, going over the same scene again and again because Crusoe shut both eyes as he fired his gun, because the sky was too cloudy, because the smoke of the cannibals' fire had been blown downwards by the wind.

One of his favourite remarks is: "Big guns cannot destroy Society so you must scare it with cruelty." The words give you the little man well enough with his wrinkled face and disquieting eye. To frighten, to express truth so that men are shaken and in the most brutal manner possible, is the aim he is for ever seeking even in his *Robinson Crusoe*. It looks as though the picture may well be banned, like *Les Olvidados*, for the under-sixteens. No shame, no claptrap, nothing but a man tortured by solitude. The struggle with nature takes second place; what comes first is man's struggle with manhood, with himself. Bunuel will not allow his Crusoe to find comfort in the Bible. Friday alone remains, and the sexual obsession, the dark uneasy moment when the savage comes out of his hut dressed as a woman.

Even in his delirium Crusoe is not allowed to escape his torturers. His father's odious, Puritan countenance rises before him, the ironical mouthpiece of the society, the life, from which he has fled.

We followed Bunuel's every scene with passionate interest and realised that he was making Crusoe do what he would have done himself in the circumstances, not what the public would like him to do. He had, however, been compelled to make his film in colour and was enraged in consequence.

"It's a waste of time!" he howled. "It makes for prettiness and I've no use for prettiness!"

He cares nothing for the marvellous, exquisitely photogenic colours of the Pacific. He infinitely prefers to remember the low haunts of Paris and the night he spent with Derain, going the round of them. Between 8 p.m. and 2 in the morning they visited sixty.

Friday was a magnificent Indian with a fine, supple, muscular body, and Crusoe was a tall, fair-haired youth, whose blue eyes could flash furiously on occasion but whose usually gentle air and deep laugh seem better suited to the role of a nice, home-keeping father of a family than that of a man fighting for his life. The local shark-fishers were recruited to impersonate cannibals and pirates. They were enchanted to go about in loin-cloths or elaborate seventeenth-century costumes, to pull canoes up on to the sands, to light fires, to fight one another with swords and yell the skies down.

Meanwhile Hollywood was furious that Bunuel should succeed where it had failed and announced the two biggest productions ever: *Mrs Robinson* and *Robinson's Son*. The Hollywood progeny of the Crusoes are not likely to have much in common with Bunuel's shipwreck.

5

Sharks by Night

EVERY afternoon we met D...., excellent man, sitting over a large plate of shell-fish which he savoured with subtle pleasure. He was passionately fond of fishing and hunting and told us tales, as he pressed his cigar between his plump fingers, of the extraordinary adventures he had undergone or witnessed. There is plenty of strong emotion to be found in Mexico whether you happen to want it or not. He had a little Indian godchild who lived in the forest, whom he often went to visit. On these occasions the family sometimes arranged lavish and dangerous boarhunts for him. One night, alone in the darkness, he detected a movement in the undergrowth. Alarmed, he raised his gun and fired. Next day a fine cow was found dead, since when the hunters of those parts sing the song of the *compadre frances que mato una vaca*.

At moonrise D.... would take us out fishing. He carried a revolver in one hand and a lantern in the other. The gear was my responsibility. We walked in single file along the seashore, beneath the coconut-trees. A sharp report: only D.... trying out his gun! We seemed utterly alone with the lapping waters. Yet, far away, there would appear a tiny, swaying light. Crouching forward like conspirators, we would creep towards it: only a loin-clothed Indian mending his nets. D...., rolling his trousers up to his knees, would wade through some rivulet rushing to its death in the great sea.

Our friend's white calves used to look whiter than ever in the pale moonlight. As we scrambled along the overhanging rocks (Aliette, giddy, crawling on all fours) the bag containing our bait —small live fish—would flap against my side and a sudden wave would soak us. Yet D.... went vigorously ahead, his plump buttocks swaying as he scrambled round the corners of the rocks. A loud "Oof!" of relief was a sure sign that the ideal spot had been reached. On one occasion when he put his lantern down on a large stone, a black shape leapt down upon it with a shrill cry and in the twinkling of an eye both lantern and dark shape disappeared. We had been plundered by a monkey.

Arranging our things about us we would cast our lines. Below us the water boiled and bubbled; from time to time phosphorescent gleams lit it up. A shout from D .... would rouse us. His line was tightening and jerking violently. Pulling on it, the rod curving, he reeled in with all his strength. A large fish appeared only to dive back again, unwinding all the precious line, so laboriously won. Ten minutes of hard fighting followed, punctuated by loud exclamations from the gallant D .... and much energetic munching of his cigar-end. At last the creature tired; a flat head emerged, sank and came up again. "A baby shark," said D .... and Aliette shrank back in alarm. The shark was dragged up on to our rock, a great flat head punctuated by minute eyes. D .... finished it off with a bullet and blows from the butt of his revolver; its endurance was really incredible.

At the risk of being carried off by a monkey, Aliette had climbed on to a further rock. The return, burdened with our catch and deprived of our lantern, was a bit difficult. D .... hummed cheerfully to himself as he trampled the sea-shells underfoot. Dawn was already breaking.

6

A Village Festival

Our honeymoon tour might well have ended here between the palm-trees and the warm sands. Time and again we found it hard to tear ourselves away from some attractive spot, lulled, almost, into forgetting our plan, the great project we believed in, did not believe in. . . .

Laden with coconuts, shod with Indian sandals (Aliette has a passion for sandals; we were to amass a considerable collection), we took the train to Tlaquepaque, where there was a fair and feast-day such as every French village celebrates once a year.

And indeed nothing was missing, neither the shooting-galleries nor the dodgems nor the swings. Every house was decorated with lamps and fairy-lights; orchestras played at every street corner; seated under the *Zocalo* arcades, thousands were enjoying their tequila, the famous Mexican brandy, sharpened with lemon-juice and salt.

Strolling musicians wandered from table to table and sang, to trumpet accompaniment, the songs that are in vogue. They look very well in their huge hats. The soldiery and the fire-brigade march past; they have some difficulty in getting through the dense crowd. At a street corner six men are doing wonders behind a *marimba*, a gigantic xylophone. They would toss their sticks into the air, each stick falling upon the appropriate note with great richness of effect. A little farther on, draped in a red and black *serape*, a blind man turned the handle of his hurdy-gurdy, grinding out *Penjamo*, the most popular tune of the moment.

The procession came down the high street. At its head strutted a fat fellow brandishing an enormous cow's head out of which rockets suddenly flew forth, describing fantastic patterns in the air before falling at the feet of the screaming spectators. A terrific

31

scuffle ensued. The Mexicans call these rockets *buscapie*, "feet-seekers". A green frock caught fire and buckets of water were poured over its wearer. Meanwhile other rockets climbed into the sky and rained down streams of many colours. Wretched little ragamuffins crawled between our legs holding up their dirty little hands for money. Beer was flowing freely; and the men fell over each other as they staggered off towards the red-light quarter where numbers of unattractive women were awaiting them perched up on odd sorts of platforms along the walls.

The rockets continued to spin through the air, giving their long whistling cry and falling down on to the crowd. It was really getting dangerous and I had no twenty-gallon hat to keep my head safe. The orchestras redoubled their volume, the blaring of the trumpets drowning the guitars; every iron-wrought balcony was draped with flowers. Far into the night, amid floods of tequila, Tlaquepaque enjoys her holiday.

1. MEXICO: In Guadalajara. Aliette has her shoes cleaned

2. MEXICO: The market in Zacatlan de las Manzanas, near Puebla

3. MEXICO: A village church, its architecture typical of the country

7

An Old French Priest
ends his Life in the
Sierra

THE French colony in Mexico is quite important.
Wherever we went we found a large and most hospitable group
of Frenchmen. Most of them originally arrived here poor from
Barcelonette but have succeeded, by hard work and grit, in becoming managers in the textile trade, in big shops, or cigarette
factories. Every year they return to France for their annual
holiday and many of them, having made their pile, settle at last
in the Basses-Alpes and show the villages how comfortable, how
often luxurious, life can be on the other side of the Atlantic.

In Mexico City, Guadalajara, Monterey, San Luis and elsewhere
they have established centres of culture, classes, lectures, schools,
films.

But every Frenchman in Mexico is not so privileged, the eighty-
year-old priest, for instance, whom we visited in the remoteness
where he lived, up in the hills, almost alone.

Zacatlan de las Manzanas is one of the little mountain villages
that are always cool. Fifty yards or so from the church is an
ancient, two-storeyed house, surrounded by high walls, the home
of the Reverend Father José Maria Pic de Belloc. An elderly lady
in a black gown received us and led us into a big room full of
curios. At the end of it stood a grand-piano and near-by, gleaming
in the shadows, a harp.

The farthest door opened and in came an elegant old gentleman in ordinary dress. He greeted us with the most charming

C   33

smile. Father de Belloc was sent out to Mexico as a missionary long before the 1914–18 War. Later, to avoid the persecution all ecclesiastics suffered in those years, he took refuge in the house of a rich Mexican, father of four daughters, who adopted him. The revolutionary authorities presumed he had gone back to France and no further search was made, yet for twenty years he never moved beyond the garden. The rich Mexican died but the four daughters remained unmarried and continued to care for their protégé. They had sworn to conceal and keep him safe. He played the harp and the piano to them in the cellar behind carefully felted doors.

All the sisters are dead now save one, the dark-robed lady who had let us in. But the priest is still, at eighty, a vigorous man and says his Mass daily in the big drawing-room. Times have changed, and there is no longer any need for him to hide. The villagers like him much better than their own priest, who detests him cordially.

In his spare time he composes music to amuse his elderly companion. Aliette begged him to play us some of it. He raised his arms in deprecation, smiled, laid down his pipe and seated himself on the piano-stool.

And what was our amazement to hear, in this remote corner of the world, written and played by an old French priest—a delightful mazurka! Waltzes and minuets and polkas followed gaily. Tears came into our eyes. Outside the window a great white horse galloped by. . . .

Father de Belloc rose to his feet, his face shining with pleasure. He made us talk to him of France and Frenchmen; he was deeply moved. But night had come; we had to depart. He gave us his blessing. Travellers from France were very rare, he said, holding our hands long in his. He came with us to the front door, and the old Mexican lady opened it with her gnarled fingers. He stood on the threshold waving to us until a donkey caravan blotted out visited and visitors.

Three days later a large white envelope arrived in Mexico City containing a gavotte dedicated to us by the padre José Maria Pic de Belloc.

8

Arizona and the Best
Sandwiches in the
Desert

ONE morning we discovered to our horror that we had only ninety-nine dollars left. If we were to eat up our capital at this rate the grand tour was done for. Our minds were soon made up. Luggage and souvenirs of Mexico were strapped on behind and we were off on our ancient Dodge, *en route* for Texas and San Francisco and the chance of a ship to the Far East.

One has to be especially careful driving over the famous Pan-American highway. Mexicans like to go fast, and every man says to himself: "I'll get past that chap!" There are constant accidents, and the culprits invariably drive on. An even greater danger is to stop and try to help a casualty; the police will swear you are to blame and if you do not pay the usual *mordida*, cash down, your kind action will be rewarded by a spell in prison. As for the victim himself, there is every chance of his being robbed, dead or alive, by the men who should be taking care of him.

At night we slept in little hotels that became progressively dearer as we approached the United States frontier. By day we drove on, pausing from time to time to eat a tortilla, stuffed with the traditional red beans.

Starting off again across the empty desert after one of these halts, I noticed a strong smell of burning. Appalled, I stopped, and jumped out. Thick smoke was coming from under the car. I grovelled on my belly and discovered, much to my alarm, that the insulation of the battery-cable was on fire. The cable ran along

35

the lead of the brake-fluid—highly inflammable stuff. It was also wound round the petrol intake. The tank was full; we might blow up at any moment. Aliette couldn't understand my sudden panic. I tore off my shirt, got down again, and tried to stifle the flames, which were still licking around the petrol pipe. I managed it at last and crawled out, trembling and covered with grease.

I took out the cable, cleaned it from end to end and wrapped it in every inch of surgical tape we possessed. Aliette took the wheel. I sat on the mudguard with my nose in the motor and we went on—not very happily.

The road runs through an eternity of desert. Every now and then an unexpected board appears in the rubble to say "Straight ahead for 200 miles". We increased our pace a little, pausing occasionally to clean the cable. Hot oil from the motor was still falling on it, drop by drop. The irritating smell of burning lingered for hours.

Sand and stone and cacti, not a single village, very rarely a car, utter solitude. . . . Vultures wheeling over the carcass of a donkey that has died of thirst. Mauve sunsets, transparent clouds of dust, here and there a crumbling yellowish mud wall on which someone has written in large capitals the name of the new President: Adolfo Ruiz Cortinez. . . . These were the last traces we saw of Mexico on the celebrated Pan-American highway. In a few days there would be greater thrills; one of the most dangerous motor races in the world was to be run on it.

No sooner were we across the frontier than we came into a mass of factories, rails, refineries. Nature has not changed, yet the landscape is totally transformed; the desert is no longer the desert. The roads are three deep in traffic in both directions, and railway lines run alongside. Thousands of telegraph poles weave their endless wires above the dry earth covered with great rocks and thick-leaved plants.

The strangest, indeed the most shocking thing if you have grown unaccustomed to it, is the multitude of advertisements that blossom in the desert. Every half mile or so are road-signs instructing the traveller in red letters on a yellow ground to "See the real Indians, the only guaranteed genuine Indians in this region", and advising him as he dashes by at top speed to "See them at work. Talk to them". Suddenly, out of the bare immensity, a petrol station crops up and a little red and yellow house. Two "genuine"

Indians, complete with feathers, squat by the door. A little farther the surfeit of advertisements begins again: "You will not only see real Indians but the biggest boa-constrictors in the world and many beasts and birds of prey." This is New Mexico, "The Land of Enchantment", according to the number-plates of the cars.

Life is getting more expensive. The men at the petrol stations are once more clean and civil, and by every pump is a tap of iced water that is delicious and, what is more, perfectly drinkable. And what a joy to munch really crisp salad in every roadside bar!

We have returned to safety, but how dull and sad it is! Alas! for the rockets of Tlaquepaque and the tottering Mexican buses hung with pictures of the Virgin! Alas! for the lilting Spanish voices. . . .

New Mexico, Arizona, States as big as France and seeming exactly alike as we drove through them on our worn tyres. . . .

The road was wide and flat, set between rows of cacti and fragments of rounded rock. Fifty, a hundred miles, and not a single house. But then, rising suddenly out of the wilderness, were two churches. On one was a luminous sign: "The Church of the Seventh Day Adventists gives better and shorter sermons than do the Presbyterians opposite." Just beyond was a yellow-washed shanty and on its roof the boldly painted words: "The best sandwiches in the desert." We drew up, got out, went through a trellised door to find ourselves in a large room hung all round with advertisements for beer and cigarettes. Flopped on rough wood stools were two vast females, both half-drunk, both dressed in khaki trousers and shirts that were much too tight for them. They were discussing the latest football results with the proprietor, a tall, weedy fellow with protruding ears. One of them noticed our accent and guessed we were French. She slewed her fat bottom round, grasped one of the six empty beer bottles lined up on the counter and grunted thickly: "You, I bet you're Frenchies. I was in France all through the War. I was a lorry driver."

She roared with laughter.

"One night near Versailles" (we had the greatest difficulty in recognising the word) "I wanted to pinch a case of brandy. I got a bullet in my leg." She pulled up her trousers and showed us the scar on her hairy calf. "I got some good friends in France," she went on. "I don't remember their names. They live near Marne. I called 'em up a few months ago from New York. I was boozed when I asked the girl on the international line to get 'em for me. Next morning I'd sobered up but when I got them I realised I didn't know a word of French and they didn't know a word of English. So all I could say was 'Bonjour'. It cost me twenty dollars."

Her companion watched her, stiff with admiration. We told her that we were going to Los Angeles, and she brought out a note-book and scribbled an address and a couple of lines: "Darling Mother. I'm sending you a sweet French couple. The Republicans have won so you can be nice to them. Kisses. Virginia."

We thanked them for their kindness and asked them what they were doing in the desert.

"Oh, we come here every year to collect dead cactus to make lampstands."

On we went. The heat was terrific, the landscape monotonous. To forget it, Aliette brought out a pocket Larousse and asked me to give the exact meaning of words picked out haphazard. We were much ashamed to find that we didn't know half of them.

Presently, at a bend of the road, I got another fright. The clutch pedal had become loose. I could no longer change gear. Once again we stopped and I crawled under the car. At first I thought that the return-spring must have broken. With our only tools— pliers and a screw-driver—I undid the spring of the emergency brake and fixed it to the pedal. No result; the pedal would not declutch. Hot oil was dripping gently on to me, and I racked my brains to picture what had happened. After an hour's struggle, we found that the clutch was uncoupled. And the desert was all about us; there was not a mechanic within a hundred miles; it was a proper breakdown. What was to be done? We should have to manage the job ourselves. Crouched on the floor between the steering-wheel and the seat, Aliette struggled painfully to hold the clutch lever in position so that I could get the rod back into the gear-box. Ten times we tried, ten times we failed. Aliette was soaked in oil and grease and was rapidly losing her temper. We were half-way on to the road, and the zip of the cars whizzing by was most disturbing.

Doubled up, my head against the right-hand wheel, Aliette hanging on for all she was worth, I pulled and pulled. The rod slipped into the tiny hole where it belonged. At last! Night had almost fallen. I emerged into the clean air completely black and enjoyed a delightful scene with my wife who chose to recall, not without melancholy, that only recently had she been considered one of the smartest women in the States. To crown our sorrows there was not a drop of water within fifty miles.

I unhooked the number plates and arranged them on the seat so as to keep my filthy clothes from blackening the cushions for good and all. We wrapped rags round the steering-wheel and started off again, perfectly conscious that our rough-and-ready repairs might give way at any moment. It was quite obvious that our only pair of pliers could not tighten bolts as they should be tightened.

9

Hollywood: Forty
Dollars easily earned

AT LAST we reached a village. There was a petrol-pump gleaming in crimson and gold and an attractive sign-board: "The most up-to-date w.c.s in the country." Down we got, and were not disappointed: lots of hot water, immaculate towels, seats treated constantly with ultra-violet rays and—for the gentlemen—an automatic machine that, says the show-card, distributes preventatives "for exclusively prophylactic use".

The street continued. Good-bye desert; we were not to see it again until we got to India. We did not know it, but we had entered the interminable suburbs of Los Angeles.

We cleaned ourselves and proceeded into this Paradise of the Film, the Wireless, and Television. For hours we wandered happily over the "Sunset Boulevard" which crosses the whole of Hollywood and ends in the sea. On either side of it, set in lovely parks, stand the world's most luxurious homes.

At every street corner boys in striped shirts sell maps showing where the great film stars live. Aliette pointed out the big, Colonial-style house surrounded by pine-trees that used to be Charlie Chaplin's; Clark Gable's is long and low and in the best modern manner, and there on the right is Gary Cooper's. Sumptuous convertibles, cream-coloured Jaguars, black or red Cadillacs, glitter in the drives.

A red light stopped us in front of the famous Ciro's, resort of all the Hollywood high-ups. But behind the display and luxury of the front streets are reasonably inexpensive hotels. We unloaded our luggage and ourselves at one of them. Stepping out on

40

our eighth floor we described our journey to the fat and smiling
negro lift-man. "Marvellous!" he cried. "You must certainly go
and talk about it on the radio——" He paused for a moment. "But
see here," he went on. "Campbell's Soups have a quiz-programme
every evening. If you answer a few questions correctly, they give
you forty dollars."

I glanced at my watch; we just had time to get to the broad-
casting station before the beginning of the programme: I grabbed
Aliette's arm and we dashed off down Sunset Boulevard, round
the corner and down Vine Street and into the long pale green
building of the NBC. An usherette in brown trousers with yellow
stripes led us into a big hall, which was full of people. Beside me
a short-sighted old gentleman was studying the programme which
is handed out to one as one enters and which gives the list of the
subjects to choose from, "Modern Novels", "Dressmaking",
"Modern Painting", etc.

The doors were closed, the lights faded, the audience started
whispering, drums rolled and a grey-haired gentleman stepped
out on to the stage. Wild applause! It was Walter O'Keefe, the
well-known actor, Radio-man No 1, who gives brilliance to many
of the most sensational advertising broadcasts. He began by
mincing delicately round the "mike", telling a little story that sent
the crowd into roars of laughter. At the end of it he glued his
mouth to the "mike", flashed his eyes splendidly and announced
that Campbell's Soups will give forty dollars to any person
answering correctly a few questions on one of the listed subjects.

The stage-set behind him was composed of huge boxes of the
said soup, brilliantly floodlit. The entire audience jumped to its
feet; everybody wanted to be questioned. This was too much, and
O'Keefe waved his hands as though in protest; there must be some
sort of selection.

"Which of you have come from a long way off?"

"New York!" "Montreal!" "Chicago!" The names resounded
from various parts of the hall.

"Paris!" shouted Aliette at the top of her voice.

The crowd turned to look. Walter O'Keefe signed to us to come
on to the stage. We did so, somewhat nervously, to a thunderous
burst of applause.

As soon as we were up a cheerful-looking little man took charge
of us. Where, he wanted to know in a confidential whisper, should

he send us a free case of Campbell's products? In the matter of addresses we were a bit nonplussed. We agreed that the best would be our old landlady in Mexico City who used to cry out whenever she saw us: "And you're going to California in that ramshackle car!"

We lined up with the other examinees and waited more and more nervously.

"Ladies and gentlemen, we have the pleasure of entertaining tonight a young French couple who are going round the world on three hundred dollars. Our Delicious Campbell's Soups have deputed me to ask them a few questions which will help them, with our best wishes, to face further adventures. They have chosen 'Modern Painting'."

We walked up to microphone, and Walter O'Keefe took us by the arm.

"A five-dollar question. Who painted 'The Burial at Ornans'?"

I hesitated; Aliette's increasing nervousness was catching.

"Courbet."

"Quite right. Curbett!" says O'Keefe.

Bravo, bravo. Loud applause.

"Now for a ten-dollar question. What is the school of painting that uses nothing but dots?"

"Pointillism!" shouted Aliette firmly.

More applause. And so it goes on until we have won our forty dollars. A golden-haired young woman handed them up to us in crisp, new notes.

O'Keefe gave us a beaming smile. "And what will you do with the money?" he asked. I was still carefully ruminating my reply when I heard Aliette's: "Fill up the tank and carry on!" The hall rocked with laughter.

"Ah ha! But tell me, lady, before we let you go off and fill your tank, which is your favourite Campbell soup?"

Aliette stammered and spluttered. I whispered "Tomato!" and nudged her arm, in an attempt to draw her attention to the huge cardboard boxes on the left. But oh dear! The nearest label said "Onion Soup" and before I could stop her Aliette cried out: "Onion and Tomato!"

O'Keefe was shaken but managed to laugh it off: "Well, dear listeners. That just goes to show we must hurry up and export Campbell's soups to Paris!"

At the end of the broadcast, after another rolling of drums, O'Keefe announced solemnly: "Just one more thing, ladies and gentlemen. Campbell's Soups are going to ask you a last question —for two hundred dollars!"

A dead silence. We shivered with excitement. O'Keefe made a face, and seizing the "mike" shouted: "How old is Einstein?"

M'm. . . . A fortune was in the balance; we could hardly contain ourselves. Seventy, was it? or seventy-five, or eighty? Aliette split the difference and answered: "Seventy-two." But we lost; he was two years older.

Out in the cool night, surrounded by the temptations of Hollywood, we fingered our packet of new notes. Next day, the Dodge's tanks filled with super-fuel, we drove on, between the vineyards and the sea, to San Francisco.

10

San Francisco: We become Salesmen in a Big Store

IT WAS pouring with rain and visibility was almost nil. Our windscreen wiper never had worked; the water dripped through the shoddy hood. However, a break in the clouds gave us a glimpse of the lovely Golden Gate bridge, its farther end lost in the mist. We had reached San Francisco, generally reckoned the most delightful city in the States. We were about to enjoy some of the best times of our whole tour.

Our big worry, though we never discussed it, was: how to cross the Pacific? We could not start to enjoy the charms of San Francisco until we had solved the vital problem of how to find a ship.

But first we had to find rooms. The French Consulate handed us our voluminous mail and kindly suggested a small, inexpensive hotel, owned by a Frenchman, in the middle of the town. We had the greatest difficulty getting there. San Francisco is all hills, and the wretched Dodge creaked and struggled and nearly boiled over. To the stupefaction of the passers-by we climbed the steepest slopes backwards. A policeman watched us with a benevolent eye. Every now and then the street rings with a terrific clangor of little bells and one of the picturesque trams of which the city is so proud dashes by.

The proprietor of the York Hotel, a giant with grey hair and an Aveyron accent, started life here, he told us, in 1902, as a poor baker. He now owns several hotels. The York looked a bit grand to us, but he slapped us on the shoulder with his large, rough

44

hand: "I always make special prices for my own people." So we found ourselves installed in a magnificent room and bathroom at a cost of only two and a half dollars—a record in America.

The next thing was to launch our attack on the shipping companies.

At the outset things did not look too good. By great bad luck—and for the first time in years, they said—every berth for Japan had been booked months ahead. The managers of the American President Line granted us an interview in their luxurious offices but they were adamant: the boats were full and they were not prepared to take a cent off their prices for all the publicity we could offer. Yet the idea of publicity seemed to interest them better than we had hoped.

There are a great number of companies; it was plain that if we had to visit all of them we should have to spend some days in San Francisco. We even tried some of the Japanese lines. Their managers were extremely courteous. They listened to us in complete silence, their faces utterly rigid, empty of the faintest hint of interest. The atmosphere was in fact so odd that I myself began to wonder what I was doing there.

Our first evenings, absolutely exhausted, we used to drop into a drugstore and have a sandwich and an ice-cream before returning to our hotel. The waitresses soon got to know us and became quite friendly.

Less unluckily we happened, quite by chance, to run into a reporter of the *Chronicle*, one of the biggest dailies. Next morning our photographs appeared together with a write-up, richly exaggerated, of our adventures.

After that the telephone started to ring without stop: "Monsieur Lapierre, I am a young American and I work in a bank. Next summer I want to see France and Europe. I haven't a cent. I should like to meet you and ask your advice."

"Monsieur Lapierre. My name is Ted Milhous. I am a young architect and my wife works at the telephone exchange. Last year we travelled through Europe much in the same way as you. Everyone was marvellous to us. We're not rich but we'd like you to know that if our room is any use to you we'd be happy to let you have it. We can always manage."

"This is Dr Goldberg speaking. My wife, my children and I all read the wonderful article in the *Chronicle* this morning. We would very much like you to come and spend Thanksgiving Day with us."

We were so touched that we accepted. A moment later a resounding "Oh!" made me jump. Aliette had discovered a girlhood friend who came out to California some while ago and married a doctor.

Dr Goldberg was a little man with a bald head and greying temples. He wore a Charlie Chaplin moustache; his voice was very gentle; he was a dentist. His wife "Minnie" was one of the best-known gynaecologists in the States, attending all the international congresses. Her eyes were dark and shining; she represented the true type of sweet-tempered intellectual and must have been very pretty.

They welcomed us more than cordially in their big house in California Street. We were particularly touched at being invited on Thanksgiving Day, which is the traditional family feast, celebrated by eating a turkey, amongst other things, in commemoration of the *Mayflower* pilgrims.

Everyone was gathered round the big table, the father and mother, the eldest son, a stage-manager to be and just finishing his studies at the University of California to that end; the daughter, passionately keen on the arts and France; the grandmother, author of the delectable dishes we were about to enjoy. Before sitting down, Minnie Goldberg lit the ritual Jewish candlestick and there was a moment of silence and self-communion.

We were never to meet a more gracious and delicately bred family. Music followed the liqueurs. Dr Goldberg was as clever with the percussion as with the Swanee Whistle. We laughed our heads off watching him accompany a record of boogie-woogie, rolling his eyes in his enthusiasm.

American hospitality, so simple, so moving, goes straight to the heart. We owe our happiest memories to these kind people and one or two others like them.

A week of steamship companies but still no ship. We did not despair, but we had only just enough cash left to pay our hotel bills; the time had clearly come to earn some more. Nothing would make us touch the envelope marked in red "Fares" and the hundred dollars inside it that we had grimly hoarded since we left New York.

So, one wet morning, we set forth. Aliette to one of the two big rival shops of San Francisco, I to the other. At the White House a kindly, smiling young woman in the Staff Personnel office instantly engaged me as a salesman; Aliette was equally fortunate at the City of Paris. There was nothing really to be surprised at; the Christmas holidays were in sight and all the shops were engaging extra assistants. Before starting work, however, we had to do some intensive training, paid of course. I was to appear, the nice young woman told me, a quarter of an hour before opening time the day after tomorrow.

The weather was lovely again. I could not help feeling a little alarmed as well as intensely curious, as I left Aliette. She, too, was on her way to be taught the art of selling, American style.

About twenty of us assembled in a big classroom. Against the light-coloured walls, blackboards stood out bearing enormous show-cards. I was the only man. To my left an elderly woman was toying with her pencil. She had admirably blued hair, and hands covered with rings. The women were of all ages. Nearly every one of them wore a wedding ring yet they invariably called each other "Miss".

A bell rang, and a young woman of about thirty entered. She had on a tight grey dress and her hair was drawn back smoothly into a chignon. She was carrying an armful of little books, neatly bound in sham leather, which she smilingly distributed. They were change-books and were full of notices explaining what to do in every possible circumstance.

The lesson began; we listened in respectful silence.

"Dear fellow workers—I say fellow workers, for the word employee is unknown in the White House—the directors have asked me to give you a little advice on your new career. But first of all I must tell you something about our splendid shop. The White House was founded at the beginning of the century by a Frenchman, Raphael Weil. Its first name was *Maison Blanche* . . ."

The history of the White House followed. Our teacher took short steps to the right, short steps to the left; she was deeply conscious of the importance of the part she was playing.

"It is an honour to work for the White House. You will soon realise that. But the great thing is to live up to that honour at every moment, in every way. To do this you must learn how to give complete satisfaction to the customer . . ."

She then delivered herself of an oration on the necessity of giving complete satisfaction to the customer. Another bell; a short break; we were invited to visit the rest-rooms that had been put at our disposal. Our young instructress took my arm and drew me towards the lift. We talked a bit. In the evenings, she told me, she went to art classes; her husband kept a restaurant; she was fascinated by my expressionless face.

The lift set us down in front of a luxurious lounge furnished with red leather arm-chairs and guarded by two Coca-Cola machines. Beyond was an elegant cafeteria so rich in salads of all kinds, vegetables, meat-dishes, fruit, sweets that I was rendered completely speechless. My new friend was much amused at my astonishment.

The second lesson was on definitely more practical lines. We had another teacher, a little woman with short, dark hair.

"To get your future customer in the best mood for buying," said she, "we cannot advise you too strongly to use 'Chlorodent' tooth-paste and to spray your armpits night and morning with 'Odorono'. Both can be bought here in the perfumery depart-ment."

No one batted an eyelid, and she went on: "Moreover, in the present damp weather, it is a good thing to powder the feet, thus diminishing perspiration."

These aesthetic considerations having been disposed of, the lights in the hall went out and a white screen was let down over the central, largest blackboard. A film operator in a white overall projected a picture entitled "The art of good salesmanship". A car was shown standing by a petrol-pump and a garage-hand ready to fill the tank.

The driver of the car: "Full right up, please."

The garage man: "With pleasure, sir."

He does so and asks: "Have you checked your oil, sir?"

The driver: "Fill her up with oil."

The garage man: "A breakdown is always tiresome. Are the sparking plugs all right?"

The driver: "Change the sparking plugs."

The garage-man: "Is the fan belt all it should be?"

The driver: "Change the fan belt."

And so on until the unfortunate driver, who had only stopped for some petrol, goes off with a new car.

4. JAPAN: Street-singers in Kyoto

5. JAPAN: A demonstration of skill by the local fire-brigade

7. JAPAN: In Nagoya, an old man makes "cloisoné" pottery

6. JAPAN: Dominique and Aliette visit a temple

We had all followed the unfolding of the plot with the closest attention, paying great heed also to our teacher's comments: "You needn't take it quite literally. You just let the principle soak well in. . . ."

So far so good. We now had to get the hang of the technical side even if we were only to be salesmen for a couple of days. I and my fellow learners had to learn the many different forms of sale: the cash sale, the sale on account, the sale with or without delivery, the sale that allows or does not allow for delivery within the State or out of it, the sale that is carriage paid and the sale that is COD, the sale that is untaxed or that carries a federal tax or a local tax, etc. . . .

Very complicated; my head swims. But the management had foreseen everything. At the end of an exhausting day we are sent away with a set of problems to be solved and brought back next morning. I found Aliette on the bed already wrestling with her home-work. By midnight, with the help of the notices in our charge-books, we were able to make out a check showing, for instance, that Mrs Tom Davis of 212 Taylor Street, Reno, Nevada, was to be sent seven pairs of stockings COD at one dollar fifty each: the snag to look out for here being that Mrs Davis did not live in California and so did not pay the local tax.

Oh! It's a great life! In no time we shall become two fully qualified sales assistants in a big American store.

After another long and difficult stage at the cash-register, I became No E 470 in the book department. My immediate boss was a plump, amiable little man who used to trot about with his hands behind his back and his round little belly well forward. He greeted me in a most kindly manner. His personal assistant was a "Miss" of uncertain age. She was a grandmother and wore her dyed fair hair combed up on top of her head. There was a salesman called Doyle, a tall, bony fellow with a 'crew-cut", to whom I took and who took to me at once so that I was able to tell him in the course of our long hours behind the counters of my shipping troubles and my hopes of further travel. The two others were a highly polished gentleman, beautifully dressed, who had been here for years and had his own special customers, and the widow of a clergyman who was quite incredibly ugly.

My first days were both painful and ridiculous. I knew practically nothing of the books on the stalls and remained by the best-

D

sellers, as they were easy and sold like hot cakes. But that can't go on for ever. My conscience troubled me when I had to advise people about things I did not know myself.

"What would you suggest for an old gentleman just out of hospital who has read all the latest novels?"

I racked my brains miserably and usually fell back on a dusty set of Malraux which I had found under the counter, or *The Wages of Fear*, or *Aphrodite*, of which I had unearthed a few dog-eared copies. Little by little, however, by looking up, between two jobs, the repeat orders, I got an idea of what was popular. To my great surprise the work most in demand by buyers of all ages was the Revised Version of the Bible.

I also managed to get rid of 1951 Christmas numbers of *L'Illustration*, which had been marked down, and of *Paris mon cœur*, though that cost twelve dollars and the customers were apt to shy at the uncommonly high price. But it was Christmas time and they bought them occasionally as presents.

My cash sales were infinitesimal. Nearly everyone had an account, and all I needed to do was to make out my bill and ask the purchaser to sign it. No check, no inquiry; the customers of the big shops can buy as they please without a penny in their pockets or any proof of identity. Everything is done on trust; it seems that frauds are very rare.

Most of the customers had no clear idea of what they wanted to buy. "I saw a book advertised in the Sunday papers," they would say, "but I can't remember its name." I had to hunt up the newspaper and find the advertisement. Sometimes the book was announced on the television, and I was completely floored. Never mind; I would sell them another instead. I specialised in a few works that I had heard praised: *The Little World of Don Camillo* and *Beyond the Himalayas* by a Judge of the High Court. I liked this one's jacket and sold as many as fifty copies a day.

Almost everyone knew I was French by my accent. Some of them even recognised me and seemed to feel that was a great feat. "Why! You're one of the young couple the *Chronicle* was talking about the other day!" I said Yes I was, and found my hand squeezed in a powerful or gentle grip: "Good luck, young man!"

There were touching episodes, as when an elderly woman came to me looking very sad and shy.

"My son has been badly wounded in Korea. I'd like to send him some books that would amuse him for Christmas but I really don't know what he'd like."

I consulted with the other salesmen, I rummaged all over the place and eventually brought her a good heap of books. As she signed her receipt she whispered: "I hope he'll never get them. I had a wire from Washington to say he may be home for Christmas." It must have been a very serious case.

Some of the customers were peculiar, like the old gentleman with dyed hair, in the elegant suit and the pearl tie-pin, who drew me aside and said: "I want a pornographic book."

I was a bit flummoxed. After a moment's thought I fetched a volume of Maillol's drawings, the best-thumbed book on the display tables. He glanced at it, grunted and handed it back with: "I want something with photographs," so I sent him to the head of the department, who might, perhaps, be able to tell him where in San Francisco such a purchase could be made.

The shop stayed open till 9 at night. At 8 o'clock I was allowed a quarter of an hour off and stretched myself out on one of the splendid red leather sofas in our rest-room. Father Christmas was there, too, every evening. We used to chat together. He was a pianist at a Chinese night haunt and always made a few extra dollars dressing up as Father Christmas. Unfortunately the shiny black boots were too small for him and the poor fellow's feet were covered with blisters.

We started work at midday and stopped, as I have said, at 9 p.m. They gave us a break of an hour for dinner and a dollar and a half to pay for it. I usually went to the shop cafeteria, which was cheaper than anywhere else and had quite the air of a smart restaurant. A quarter of an hour before closing-time I began to make up my accounts, that is to say get muddled, make mistakes and finally go to the head of the department. He would take a quick look at the total, which was often over 300 dollars a day.

The mornings were given up to finding a ship. If I made a mess of my shop accounts it was because there was only one thought in my head: that ship! A cargo-boat offered to take me on as a cabin-boy; Aliette could have gone as a stewardess on a Swedish liner, but there were no passages anywhere for the "young couple . . ."

Our worry did not prevent us from having a wonderful time. One Sunday we went to Stanford University and saw the world's biggest electron accelerator; we went to the University of California and gave a lecture; we appeared on television in a programme called French Cancan; we had tea with Darius Milhaud and spent wonderful hours with a number of friends.

In her big shop Aliette, at first, was not too comfortable. Her job was in women's underwear. She could hardly keep her face straight when a terrible old spotty-cheeked female, watching her companion try on a house-wrap, cried out: "Darling, you look too ravishing!"

The head of the department was a sour old maid. She became jealous of Aliette's popularity and insisted on her transfer. Aliette was put among the handbags and umbrellas but she was naïve enough to mention that she had been transferred, so her fate was sealed from the outset. Worse still, in her new department the handbags carried a 20 per cent federal tax whereas the umbrellas did not, which led to mistakes and sometimes considerable overcharging. Toys were then suggested, but Aliette, exasperated, refused.

The situation was saved, nevertheless, by a telephone call from "Ties", who wanted an extra assistant urgently. This time Aliette struck lucky; the head of the department fell for her at sight and all was well.

But neither of us had the least intention of making shops our life-work. A French friend, the manager of a big commercial house, who had been very kind to us from the beginning, advised me to pay one more visit to the directors of the American President Line, and in despair I went. The *President Cleveland* was sailing in a couple of days; it was our last chance.

Once again I sat in the anteroom, waiting, horribly nervous, amidst a flutter of secretaries. In an attempt to steady myself I talked to a nice little blonde typist who was busy sending out Christmas cards picturing the cathedral of Rheims. The place itself is like a crossroads; red, green, and yellow lights proclaim that the bosses are telephoning, or busy with a customer, or ready for the next one. The gentleman I was concerned with had had his light on red for an hour. But click! At last it turned green.

As I entered his office he rose. His wrinkled face looked very weary.

"I'm sorry," he said. "The *Cleveland* is full."

He sat down again adding: "But if two passengers happen to cancel their reservations I can take you. I'll charge you only one fare. I'll ring you at the White House."

My heart was in my boots. I went back to the book counters, I took my stand at the farthest end of the department so as not to hear the telephone ringing, ringing, ringing... I set myself to catch every customer in sight. By the middle of the afternoon I had done better than my 300 dollars' worth; my eagerness to sell books became a devouring passion; I even managed to land an old maid with spiritualistic leanings with four huge volumes on India and Yoga.

At 6 o'clock the head signalled to me and I knew instantly what he meant. The telephone! Leaving fifty dollars I was about to put into the till to float where they would I made a dash for it, diving past an old gentleman who looked quite shocked: "Yes, yes. Lapierre speaking."

"Hullo, Monsieur Lapierre. Get ready to sail the day after tomorrow. You can call for your tickets to Yokohama tomorrow." I rushed home to tell Aliette the good news. She took it coolly: "Don't let's shout till we've got the tickets."

Actually, when it came to adding up our cash, we found we were still a long way out. There was still the car, but it was so old! What would we get for it? and from whom?

A really nice business man we met casually at a cocktail party offered to buy it. I asked 200 dollars and to our utter stupefaction he accepted. Aliette could not help wondering—aloud—why he should want the ancient Dodge when he already had such lots of lovely cars.

He told her quite simply: "You see I'm a freemason. One of our most important duties is to help travellers. By buying your car I can tell my superiors that I have helped travellers, and, thanks to you, I shall have the chance of going up a step."

We thanked him profusely. So that Aliette might shout with joy as soon as possible, I went off at once to buy the tickets. Also to get the names and addresses of the two who had cancelled their journey, as I wanted to send them flowers.

Back at the White House to say good-bye, the sight of Doyle's incredibly thin body, conscientiously bent over an invoice, made me sad. In the days I spent selling the Revised Version to people who wanted to know my opinion of it, my only thought was to get away. Now that I was going, I felt almost sorry to leave this book department that I had known for such a little while.

Last farewells to all our friends; a perfect evening with the Goldbergs, whom we left with tears in our eyes. Final ice-cream at our drugstore. One of the waitresses cried out, "Happy Christmas!" and produced, from under a pile of sandwiches, a small pink box. It contained a china negro, his belly a mustard-pot, his head a salt-cellar.

For the last time we drove through San Francisco in the old Dodge; for the last time I switched on the ignition and then handed the key over to its new owner. The hum of the engine died away. Good-bye, dear old car.

The *President Cleveland* stood out clearly beyond the sheds of the harbour. She was a big grey and white ship; her funnels were painted red and white and adorned with a white eagle.

The quay-side seethed with activity. An orchestra discoursed sentimental airs, whilst the long yellow taxis drove up, disgorging sheaves of flowers, pots of plants, and passengers.

Ted, our architect friend, was here with his wife Barbara, laden with presents. Once again we were deeply touched.

Time was nearly up. Loudspeakers were warning the non-passengers to go ashore; Sisters of Mercy kissed each other; armfuls of bouquets were still being rushed on board; from the decks floated endless coloured streamers, finally creating a thick screen of paper between the bulwarks and the wharf. People were shouting and running to and fro; the orchestra played louder than ever. The gangway glided away like a monster caterpillar and disappeared. We were so high up that the faces on shore and the waving handkerchiefs already seemed remote. The *Cleveland*'s sirens bellowed. Slowly, propelled by some invisible force, we moved off. Barbara and Ted were no more than spots, than specks that we imagined rather than saw. A few moments later the whole town became visible, looking a little like Istambul, with the old tower and the houses rising up and up the hills and shining in the sun. We passed under the Golden Gate, and in the lovely after-

noon beneath a bright blue winter's sky, the land vanished. Good-
bye America.

For us, pressed close together against the rail of the glass-
roofed promenade-deck, it was the beginning of a great adventure.

11

Cocktails at Honolulu

THE third class was kept for the yellow races, there was no second, and so it was in the luxurious first that Aliette and I travelled. The big liner's five hundred passengers embraced every specimen of humanity: shopgirls going to Japan to join their fiancés; a bevy of missionaries of every religion off to some obscure corner of the Philippines or elsewhere; the Canadian Ambassador *en route* to take up his duties in Tokio; elderly ladies covered with jewels out for adventure; stout business men alert to recover their Far East markets.

This crossing happened to coincide with the Christmas holidays, and the company was making a cruise of it; most of the passengers were only making the round trip. To celebrate the religious services a Rabbi, a Protestant clergyman and a Roman Catholic priest had been called upon. The Rabbi was a ping-pong champion; the clergyman walked the decks eternally with one of his seven children; the priest smoked innumerable evil-smelling cigars. He was a plump little man, a Monseigneur no less, who wore ordinary clothes including rather loud shirts that kept ruckling up above his flannel trousers. On windless days you could track him by the smell of his cigar, even before Early Mass, which was supposed to be celebrated at seven but never began before seven-thirty.

One evening a game of *Petits Chevaux* was set up in the big saloon, and he came running in, panting with haste, plunked down his invariable cigar-box and trotted off to buy his chips. Tickled, I couldn't help asking him: "But Monseigneur! I seem to remember that the Church forbade games of chance?"

"Games of chance?" said he, shifting his cigar from one side of his mouth to the other. "What about them, so long as I do nobody

56

any harm?" The last words were accompanied by a look that added clearly: "What business is it of yours, anyway?"

But I was obstinate. "No harm? Surely if I lose my stake and you win it, my money is going into your pockets?"

He roared with laughter. The bell announcing the start of the race broke off the conversation.

On Christmas night the Captain invited us all to a monster cocktail party. We put on our best clothes and absorbed champagne cocktails and snacks till we were almost ill, and the old ladies gave the Captain such smacking kisses that his cheeks were red with lipstick. After that there were dinner and a Christmas tree and a heart-stirring psalm on the organ and the recital of a long, long Christmas story, and a ball with showers of confetti and Midnight Mass.

Next day we came in sight of Honolulu. Two long spits of land, a tall tower looming above the boats in the harbour, and we were alongside. Hawaiian dancers and musicians awaited us on the quay, twisting their bodies to the languorous strains of their guitars. Directly the gangway was run out, they glided on board and hung wreaths of flowers round our necks. Behind them came the journalists who, greatly to our surprise, singled out Aliette and myself. Pencil in hand, mouths greedily open, they bombarded us with questions: How much money had we got? What did we think of the Korean War? What were we going to do in Japan? After the reporters the camera-men. Our Monseigneur, flabbergasted, gave us his blessing.

At last we were free. A voice behind us murmured discreetly: "M. Lapierre?" I turned to meet a roundabout, bald-headed person whose nose and eyes were almost lost in his fat cheeks. It was the agent from the French Consulate. He had been warned of our arrival and welcomed us heartily, embracing us on both cheeks and hanging further garlands about our necks. We were overwhelmed by so much kindness. The first greetings over, he whirled us off in his blue convertible to the famous Waikiki beach.

Waikiki is indeed all that it is advertised to be: a blue sea leaping over coral reefs and breaking on an immensity of golden sand, palms and lovely women, smooth lawns and handsome restaurants overlooking the water. We walked up and down for quite a time, watching the people in their bare feet and bright shirts. It was all very pleasant. At the Grand Hotel, which is rust-coloured and battlemented like a Berber palace, they were harvesting coconuts. A small man, bare-footed and naked to the waist, climbed to the top of the thin, immensely tall trunks, a knife between his teeth. Below, the hotel-manager, in a shirt decorated with palm-trees, was talking into a microphone, telling the visitors about the operation, which seemed to be more of a circus turn than a matter of fruit-picking. He offered three weeks' free board and lodging to anyone who could do it. No one stirred, but we all seized on the falling nuts and enjoyed them as soon as an attendant had cut them in half. Such a delicious drink!

After that came the dancers. They wore loin-cloths and very small brassières made out of fibre, and each one carried in her long arms a tamtam or a *maraccas* for the samba. I liked some of their faces, but Aliette says their legs were too short. They sang and swayed their bodies; the undulating movement of the arm being wonderfully beautiful. One by one each performed a solo, which the others accompanied squatting on their fibre mats.

We were taken to lunch at the Country Club, an enchanting place. The hills rise behind and in front of us stretched a vast green lawn: farther off, the blue of the sea.

After lunch our host suggested a visit to Pearl Harbour which we accepted with alacrity.

Pearl Harbour is white and grey. Prodigious dry-docks that can take two aircraft-carriers at a time, battleships from Korea. Endless warehouses overflowing with every imaginable material, huge graving docks, etc, etc. . . . No trace of the Japanese bombing remains. The sunken ships have disappeared; the whole fantastic place has been rebuilt; it is now the naval base for the Korean War and for repairs. As far as the eye can see everything is in impeccable order; not a coil of rope, not a gun-turret but is tidily numbered. Gangs of men are busy remounting guns, repainting, resoldering. And a few miles from this terrific industry, from the boats that have just returned and are going back to battle, America peacocks it on her golden sands, unconcerned, at ease.

The day ended with a cocktail party given by our host and his wife in their bungalow above the bay. All the leading lights in the business life of the island were present with their wives and daughters, superbly built young blondes who looked quite charming in their light frocks. The drink flowed steadily. We sat round the Christmas tree, which was encased in a wall of Christmas cards—an old American custom. The excitement and the laughter heightened. Our round-bellied host in his shirt-sleeves left us for a moment, and returned with four little ukeleles which were instantly snatched up by the guests. A girl, kicking off her shoes, began to dance and to sing very softly. To the music of the ukeleles and of humming voices, her arms writhed like serpents; above her long legs and the regular beat of her feet, her body undulated, slow and snake-like. A spell was on us; the entrancing rhythm, the drinks, the extraordinary softness of the air, all combined in creating an atmosphere of care-free languor. The sun was setting beyond the harbour, a thousand lights twinkled on the ships. A dark young woman in a white dress told me the story of her many loves and called me "Nicky". Whenever I said anything, her eyes—large and blue and curiously shy—gazed back into mine and she murmured in a voice I no longer felt to be ridiculous, "Nicky, oh! Nicky . . . the way you speak and the way you look are just like Him." Whereupon she snuggled up closer and put her arms round me.

At my feet Aliette was talking to a young man in a very gaudy tie who was already addressing her as "Darling!" The songs and dances continued in an atmosphere of enchantment. Fortunately our ship was to sail in a few minutes, for we were by now far gone in surrender to the charms of Hawaii. . . .

Feeling decidedly "happy", we went back through the cool night to the *Cleveland*, whose sirens were already hooting. It was a lovely evening. Our new friends had bought dozens more garlands and kissed us as they put them over our heads. My little American pressed my lips and clung to me passionately. Whisky and twinkling lights, sirens, and the scent of flowers. . . .

The gangway was being raised as we climbed on board. From the bridge I threw streamers towards our charming friends of a day and, as we moved away from land, I cast into the water a necklace of flowers, as custom decrees we must do if one ever wishes to return. Soon Honolulu was but a speck on the horizon.

12

Yokohama and only
Nineteen Dollars Left

AFTER an uneventful and often very boring fortnight's journey, the *President Cleveland* sailed into the mists of Yokohama. It was bitterly cold and an icy wind swept the deck. The ship passed a number of big docks, turned and finally berthed by the appropriate quay. Behind a row of white barriers stood dim figures wrapped to the eyes in long dark cloaks. We watched them curiously but with a slight constriction of the heart; the carefree days of the crossing were over; a new life lay before us. We were at the world's end and had only nineteen dollars left. How would we fare?

It was really terribly cold. The faces on the quay could now be distinguished, and I was astonished to recognise Bob Nichyama, a young Japanese student with whom I had made great friends at my American University. He had seen us too and was waving his arms in greeting. We no longer felt quite so lonely. During the War Nichyama was one of the "suicide pilots" sent to deal with the more difficult and important targets. One day he shot down an American fighter plane in flames and killed the pilot. After the War the parents of the dead airman sent for him and with unprecedented generosity gave him the necessary thousands of dollars to attend an American university and learn the meaning of democracy. For four years Bob was a model pupil in the faculty of International Relations. He lived in one of the little houses reserved for ex-soldiers. His young wife was with him and his little five-year-old daughter and his son Yokinobu who was born in the States. The first day I went to see him I was confronted by the

60

smiling photograph of the man he had killed. I couldn't help showing astonishment. "But no," he said in a serious voice, "it isn't hypocrisy. It's just to remind me I'm not here to enjoy myself. . . ." He has never had much money and would be able to understand our predicament better than anyone.

A long procession of immigration officers came on board. They were extremely civil and welcomed us with the utmost courtesy. And, once again, the journalists! A little man with a shaven head and pure gold teeth asked Aliette why she had come to Japan. As a professional, she answered: "The big French and American dressmakers are interested in Japanese materials, in the silks and in the workmanship. I have come to get ideas that I can adapt to Western fashions."

The reporter made a note, lifted his head high, bowed, straightened himself, sucked in his breath with a hissing noise and vanished. Little did we know that Aliette's words were to bring us almost a fortune!

So we landed on Japanese soil with our ten bags and valises. Bob pointed out that it was unpardonable to travel with so much luggage. The husband of a fellow passenger laughed a lot at our dismay and offered to take us and our belongings in his big Chrysler.

Tokio was about twenty miles off. We drove down a long avenue lined with low grey shacks that were covered with coloured signs and characters but otherwise did not seem very exotic. The street, as seen from between four tightly packed bags, was nothing but cyclists, small carriages, horse-drawn carts, and uneven paving. At every corner policemen in blue uniforms and helmets with chin-straps jerked their short arms, directing the extraordinarily confused and dangerous traffic. The cyclists, in particular, had an exasperating tendency to zigzag all over the road. We were to learn later that in the matter of cars they and the foot-passengers follow a code that is personal and peculiar: "If he sounds his horn he has seen me. If he has seen me he won't run me down. So I'll just go ahead."

Without any break or transition we were in Tokio. The scene had not changed, the same dirty shacks, end to end, occasionally broken by a railway line or a gasometer. Suddenly a little man with an absurd, round, gaping-mouthed face, who had been cycling beside us, swung without a sign of warning across our path. Our chauffeur swerved violently to avoid him but the little man was caught and sent spinning. The chauffeur got out and, going towards him, stopped and bent forward, his hands on his thighs. The little man, who had jumped to his feet, walked up to him, his face scarlet with rage, stopped and bent forward in like fashion, his hands on his thighs. He then picked up his bike, dusted himself, and, adjusting his glasses, rode off. The performance lasted three minutes and not a word was spoken.

Presently houses appeared on every side. We had reached the centre of the town and were driving past the moat and the big park that surround the Imperial Palace. Our obliging friends put us down at the Teito Hotel, one of the cheapest in the capital. But four thousand yen a day for the room only! Four thousand francs! It was a catastrophe. At that rate we could not last a week in Japan.

Bob saved the situation. "I've only one room and it is very uncomfortable, but we can share it. Meanwhile let's go and put your luggage in my office."

13

Our First Evening in Japan

IT IS a tradition in Japan that, for the feast of the New Year, the head of every business should give a dinner in his employees' honour. The man for whom Bob worked was giving his dinner that night and we were also invited.

A dense crowd hurried along the broad pavements of the *Ginza*, Tokio's most famous avenue, which reminds one of the Champs-Élysées and the Grands-Boulevards. The shop-fronts were brilliantly lit and there were specially large gatherings around those where television was being shown, for it was a new thing in Japan. On the other side of the road, on top of a cinema, a monster Gerard Philippe brandished the sword of *Fanfan la Tulipe*. A few GIs went by on the arms of the little Japanese ladies known as *Pan-Pan*. The crowd poured down into the Underground; its entrances reminded me of some of the suburban Paris underground lavatories. The noise was deafening—motor-horns, screeching of brakes, terrific back-firing.

We turned into a narrow street lit by round, coloured lanterns. Every shack was a bar, full of men and men only. Sometimes one saw a group going towards a little Shinto temple, set in its delicately planned garden. Presently we arrived at a real, two-storeyed house. Bob opened the sliding door and we went into a long narrow room. A young woman in a red and violet kimono stepped smilingly forward, bowing. We took off our shoes and could only manage to insert a frozen big toe into the tiny slippers she offered us. In single file, very carefully, for the touch of a single finger would bring down the walls, we climbed a twisted,

63

highly polished wooden staircase. On the first floor we found ourselves in a small passage surrounded by paper partitions and the
sound of hidden laughter. Another sliding door closed behind
us, and we were in a little smoke-filled room where our fellow-
guests awaited us. They were all Bob's fellow clerks who were
squatting round a low table. At its head was their boss, a pleasant-
faced young American who rose and received us very kindly. The
women were in their native kimonos, the men in European dress.
The conversation rattled on at a great pace in Japanese—jerky,
monosyllabic and interspersed with whistling intakes of the
breath. Black lacquer bowls were put before us containing
delicious-smelling fish soup. The right thing to do is to drink it as
noisily as possible. A little serving-maid crouched behind each of
us, pouring out warm *sake*, the rice spirit that is the national drink.
After the soup other maids tripped in, carrying trays laden with
dishes of various sorts of raw fish, delicately cradled in lettuce
leaves, and presently relays of dishes of fried fish that had to be
dipped in soya sauce and conveyed to the mouth with chopsticks.
And eaten, once again, as noisily as may be. We had some trouble
at first with the chopsticks. From time to time sharp cries rang
out; it was Aliette dropping a well-sauced bit of fish on to her
smart skirt.

Liberally washed down by *sake*, the feast went on. It ended
with bowls of plain rice, a low-down form of food that must not
be eaten with other dishes. As we struggled with our chopsticks,
we admired the way the table was arranged, the shape and colour
of the dishes, the red and black lacquer bowls. The delights of the
eye were as carefully studied as the delights of the palate.

But oh! we were cold! My fingers were numb and so were my
feet. Aliette's eyes widen despairingly; she is equally frozen. The
room is not heated, the walls are of paper. Guests sometimes
stretch out a hand to the *hibashi*, an earthenware pot in which a
few scraps of charcoal are dying. People in Japan content themselves with getting the chill off their finger-tips. A few modern
restaurants provide foot-warmers.

Nothing on the walls. In one corner is an alcove called a
tokonoma. It used to be the sleeping-place. The rest of the floor is
bare—plain boards strewn with mats, *tatamis*. There may be one
or several, all of a fixed size. A room is said to be "so many
tatamis". Nowadays the alcove is little more than a kind of glory-

hole where screens or ornaments are stored away. The guest of honour must always sit with his back to it.

A garden is absolutely essential to every self-respecting Japanese. If the land is lacking, miniature trees and plants are grown in pots; the very poorest cultivate them. That hundred-year-old pine-tree over there, or the gnarled and twisted cherry, has been handed down from generation to generation.

Outside, snow has begun to fall. To avoid it, we follow Bob into the "Showboat", the biggest night-club known to man. It is four storeys high. On each floor are galleries opening on to a central courtyard, and in the courtyard is an orchestra, mounted on a moving platform that goes up and down, playing before each gallery in turn. The drinks—beer and cocktails—trundle in on little railed trucks and are snatched up and handed out by "hostesses" in white tulle dresses with red carnations in their hair. The din is unbelievable; nothing is so noisy as a Japanese crowd enjoying itself.

Out in the street again the snow is still falling. We fight through a positive storm to get a taxi. When found, it knocks and squeaks and hoots furiously, running at terrific speed over unexpected ruts in the grand avenue. The snow comes in through its broken windows. Aliette, whom I am doing my best to protect and keep warm, sighs for America and the comfort we have grown accustomed to. We reach the suburbs and wander for a long while in and out of criss-cross alleys, deep in mud and totally unlit. At last we stop before a little house that smells oddly of fish. We go in and take off our shoes. A glass door slides open; this is the room Bob lives in, alone at the moment, his wife and children being away.

Another sliding glass door, a little passage, the communal bathroom. There is a basin, a minute gas geyser and over it an immense wooden tub covered with boards, the famous Japanese *ofuro* that Westerners love so in cold weather. Round about six of an evening, every Japanese family fills the tub with boiling water and, having first washed carefully, climbs in and sits immersed up to the neck. Guests are always allowed first dip. But we are so late, the whole neighbourhood must have been in the murky water! It is still hot, however, so hot in fact that when I dip in a rather disgusted toe, I snatch it out again instantly; it takes me half an hour to stand my soaking. I come out scarlet, but

E

so warm that I don't feel the icy temperature of the passage and the bedroom. Aliette can't make out how the Japanese don't all die of heart failure.

Still in our overcoats, we remove the bed's top mattress. Bob will take that, and we will sleep on the box-spring underneath. Our knees to our chins, wrapped up to the eyes, we embark on our first night in Japan. The storm is still raging; wind and snow lash the windows. By morning Aliette's bottle of shampoo is a solid block of ice.

14

First Impressions

THE greatest difficulty in Tokio is to find your way about. How can you in such a huge, sprawling city where every street and every alley is exactly like its fellow? Not to mention the matter of language. But the Japanese themselves get lost. No street has a name and no house a number. All you can do is ask for the street that goes from one well-known point to another.

Our usual means of getting into town every morning was an elderly bus. (We had to save money; we had only ten dollars left.) At the beginning, to go to dine at the French Embassy in full evening dress, we took a taxi, but that was a devastating experience. Japanese drivers are the most dangerous of men; at every moment we expected the cab to fall to pieces. In our bus we could sit and watch the people at our leisure. Our first surprise was the sight of the people with colds, for if you have a cold in Japan you must put a white mask over your nose and mouth, held in place by straps over your—usually protruding—ears. Every passenger reads his paper. The Japanese press is very important; the *Asahi*, the biggest daily, is printed in three towns and has a circulation of over four million copies. Others reach two or three. The bus conductress is always a stout woman with very pink cheeks. She wears olive-green trousers and a sort of forage cap and wanders vaguely up and down, handing out her different coloured tickets and delivering a running comment in a high, wailing voice. The word "thank you" is heard on every hand (in Japan one has to repeat it three times). After a while we came to understand these monotonous mewings.

"Ladies and gentlemen, we have just passed *Shibuya Station*. Thank you very much. The next stop, if you please, is *Meguro*.

Thank you very much. And here on your right is the *Meiji Park*. Thank you very much." And so on and so on.

Most people are dressed like Europeans; only a few women keep to the kimono and the *geitas*, the high strapped wooden sandals. The men's clothes are nearly always shabby, their shoes unpolished, their shirts and collars doubtfully clean. And that at all income-levels. Many an editor of high standing, many a big business man looked to us like a poor clerk. And they all prefer dark, drab colours so that the general effect is depressing.

Once in town we went straight to Bob's office, which is in a grand new building, worthy of Madison Avenue. We had made it our headquarters for letters and telephoning, for trying to find solutions to our financial problems.

Managers and editors received us most warmly. We would sit in reception rooms on somewhat worn chairs. Occasionally small gas-stoves were lit, otherwise we had to thaw our fingers over the *hibashi*. We—I and the man I had come to see—would bring out our cards (I had had one done in Japanese) and lay them before us. Ten minutes of polite conversation, which had nothing whatever to do with the matter in hand, would follow either in halting English or in French. Very slowly, after long silences, long spells of what looked like inspired self-communion, heavy breathing, much twiddling of fingers and sips of unsweetened green tea, the gentleman would come down to business. A civility which was frequently exasperating required that our talk should be conducted without that nasty, brutal realism which makes Western conversations so coarse. There was never a definite "No" to clear the situation, always "Yes", which meant nothing and could be most baffling to the uninitiated.

"Do you think you can publish an article of this sort?" "Yes." "Will you publish it soon?" "Yes." "Do you feel it needs changing and adapting to Japanese taste?" "Yes."

A long discussion on what should be changed would follow, completely altering the meaning of the first "Yes". At last I would ask: "In fact this article is quite unwanted?" and in reply would get a "Yes" and a smile so wholly natural that it was plain that my interlocutor was marvelling at my ever having been uncertain of his original intentions.

The interviews the journalists got from us on arrival were finally published. Aliette was astonished to see a photograph of herself with her hair done in Japanese style, stiff and flat over the ears with a straight fringe. A people who can grow an oak in a flowerpot can do wonders with photographs.

Telephone calls followed rapidly and meetings were arranged.

One morning a little gentleman paid us a visit. He wore a beret and a navy-blue suit that was far too small for him; his tie was so crumpled that it was obvious that he took it off without unknotting it. Shyly he put down his visiting card: Mr Imaida, chief reporter of the *Soen Magazine*. His English was particularly bad, and we had the greatest trouble finding out what he had come about. While Aliette carried on as best she could, I slipped out and asked one of the secretaries: What is the *Soen Magazine*?

"*Soen!*" she says. "*Soen!* You don't know *Soen*? Why it is the biggest fashion magazine in Japan. It has a sale of seven hundred thousand!"

I went back to the office. The little man was taking short puffs at the long Pall Mall cigarette which Aliette had given him.

"As far as I can make out," she said, "his editor has read in the papers that I am a fashion editress. He wants me to design a collection of dresses for a dressmaking firm and to lecture on fashion at a school of dressmaking, that also belongs to him. If we accept he will come tomorrow with a contract."

I looked at him and drew in my breath with a whistling sound. Throwing my head back and taking another breath I said, "Yes," without betraying the least sign of excitement.

15

How Aliette became a Professor

HE CAME back next day with an interpreter who could jabber a bit of broken French and had enormous tortoise-shell glasses and three gold front teeth—a peculiarly ugly man. But the contract explained and confirmed yesterday's proposal:

"Madame Lapierre and *Soen Magazine* agree to the following: that a collection shall be designed in collaboration with the firm *Yoda*; that Madame Lapierre shall give the same lecture three times once a week to the pupils of the dressmaking school; that *Soen Magazine* shall have exclusive photographic rights."

Having read the contract with the closest attention we were asked the great question: "What are your terms?"

We had spent the night over them. Before answering, Aliette, suddenly transformed into the perfect business woman, pointed out that work of this kind would alter all our plans and keep us in Japan much longer than we had intended. The little man nodded his head without interruption, but remained silent.

And then I butted in and asked a really big sum. The little man appeared quite unmoved. In the best Oriental manner and with the utmost courtesy, he promised to speak to his editor and give us an answer the next day. In Japan business is always done slowly and it is the greatest mistake to show haste.

He turned up punctually the following morning. Our only concern was: "Is it Yes or No?" but he gave nothing away. We just talked and talked. Mostly about Paris. He had never been there, yet he knew the place by heart and when he asked us: "Where do you live?" and Aliette, much amused, answered: "Boulevard Pereire," he produced a greasy map from his pocket and ran his finger up the Champs-Élysées, down the avenue de la Grande-Armée and finally arrived at exactly the right spot. We gaped at him, amazed. Then, without a syllable of transition, he told us that *Soen* had accepted our terms and would send a car that afternoon to take us to the head office to sign the contract.

The car was a luxurious Chevrolet. In it we drove across Tokio to a big wooden structure, built on three sides of a courtyard. We were taken into the president's office, which was large and cold and dark. The Electric Company's water supply was running low and the current was cut off for several hours a day.

The president was small and plump, almost bald and—for a Japanese—fairly well dressed. He smiled and we exchanged a great quantity of bows, before he invited us to seat ourselves in the vast, again rather shabby, arm-chairs that had been arranged in a neat semi-circle. We were introduced to Mr and Mrs Yoda, the heads of the dressmaking business that was to make Aliette's models. Madame was rather common but very charming; her husband looked more like a commercial traveller than a big dressmaker. They chatted among themselves in Japanese and we drank green tea in little grey porcelain bowls.

Night had fallen before we even approached the business that had brought us all there. Yet we did, finally, achieve it. The contract stipulated that Aliette's work should start in a fortnight and last a month. Half the fee was to be paid immediately on signature of the contract. By candle light we wrote our names and received a bundle of notes that was, to us, a fortune. It is true that, since we left New York, the meaning of the word "fortune" had shrunk considerably. We drove back to our icy home in the handsome Chevrolet.

We did not know our Japanese friends were to try to twist that contract in scores of different, subtle ways, affording us a unique opportunity of studying the Japanese mind. That night we did not bother about anything. Our one idea was to see more of this beautiful country. We packed a bag, all ready to jump next morning into the first train that would take us to the south.

16

Touring the Land of the Rising Sun

WE TRAVELLED second class in a train that was like all American and some English trains—long coaches but no separate carriages. Behind us a Buddhist priest was conscientiously drinking green tea. To our left a man who looked the perfect type of white-collared clerk was doing his accounts with an inspired air. Opposite to him a chubby fellow dandled a small, pink-faced child that stared at us in great astonishment. Farther off, two GIs were smoking their pipes and talking to a couple of Japanese officers. Fujiyama, white against the blue sky, followed us for a long while. At its feet the cramped valleys ran up, their sides studded with wooden chalets much stained by the rain, and their hollows planted with countless little square rice-fields. Here and there you saw an old man bent over his ploughshare, scratching painfully at the soil. No meadows, never a stretch of open country, nothing but these square snippets of land spread in every direction, sometimes covered with snow and scored by narrow water-channels. A true Japanese print. Sad and leafless, the skeleton trees stood out starkly. Green box-trees, glinting with red, strangely contorted, grew on the lower hills, which were also cultivated. Not one inch of ground was wasted. In every gap, in every tiny plain, huddled a village, its roofs dark in the winter sunshine.

In the coaches loudspeakers told us where we were. They were on the platforms too, screaming away, and their comically harsh, squeaky voices mingled with the voices of the swarming crowd that tapped at our windows, seeking to sell us large and most decorative

72

brown stoneware pots of tea. The contents of the pots provoked much joy and sucked-in hissing noises among the passengers. We were also offered tangerines in string bags and hard-boiled eggs and sandwiches enveloped in cellophane and boxes about the size of chocolate boxes inscribed with black and red characters. Out of curiosity I bought one and found that it contained in neat compartments, rice, a piece of fish, scraps of meat, a highly spiced lettuce leaf wrapped round slices of cucumber, and, in a dainty wrapper, chopsticks.

All this suggested a concern for cleanliness that was rather astonishing and in complete contrast to the dirt of the people about us. They spat and belched; and ate grossly, chucking their eggshells and peel on the floor, although the string bag provided them with a paper container specially designed for refuse. These dirty ways must be quite usual, for trousered women were constantly about, sweeping up the rubbish which had constantly accumulated. The Japanese never stopped eating.

Punctually to the minute we arrived, covered with soot, at Nagoya. Nagoya has become an important harbour and the fourth biggest town in Japan. The population is over a million. Since the thirteenth century it has been the chief centre for pottery and porcelain; the first kiln was built here; seventy per cent of the china sold in the remotest corners of Mexico and Afghanistan comes from this centre.

It is, among other things, the great producer of "cloisonné", the famous enamel ware. Nobody knows exactly whence cloisonné originated but very old pieces, doubtless brought from China, are still preserved at Nara.

A toothless little man, wearing a large beige scarf, took us over his factory. It is the oldest in the city. Half a dozen men of various ages (young men are hard to find nowadays for this excessively precise and delicate work) squat in a big studio and mould the copper into the required shape—vase, pot or plate—and coat it with enamel. In a second room three men apply their design of flowers, birds, fish, and so on. The piece is then taken to an old man of eighty-four (he was in Paris, we are told, for the 1937 Exhibition), who is perhaps one of the last workers in this extraordinarily delicate craft. With metal-rimmed glasses on the tip of his nose, tiny pincers in hand, he spends ten hours a day outlining each detail of the designs with gold or silver wire so that the whole surface with its "cloisons", or little, picked-out divisions, looks like lace. The pattern is often very complicated and may take weeks. A first baking follows, after which powdered colours are spread over the little divisions and the piece is baked again for ten minutes at nine hundred degrees Centigrade. Another thin coat of enamel is added before three final firings. Last of all come hours of hand-polishing to get the surface perfectly smooth.

We wanted to photograph all these processes but everything went wrong; the flash failed in one camera and the film stuck in the other and we gave it up with great loss of face.

Although the Westernised hotel where we passed the night is the best in Nagoya it would be considered third class in America or Europe. We were much disappointed at not staying at a Japanese inn but the cold made them impossible.

Our room cost two thousand francs a day and, of course, underneath the clean bedspread, the sheets were dirty. The staff, from the manager to the smallest page-boy, were supremely amiable. Each was more zealous, more obliging, more refined than the other. The chamber-maid, when we left next morning, seemed heartbroken.

17

Hiroshima and the Largest Cathedral in the World

BEFORE going on to Hiroshima by way of the exquisitely beautiful Inland Sea, we listened to a lecture given at the French Institute in Kansai by a Dominican Father on "Sacred Art in France". The Reverend Father talked at some length of Matisse and the chapel at Vence and "its simplicity which is so near to the simplicity and bareness of Japanese Art and the Japanese aesthetic theory that the great thing, say, about a vase, is not the containing shell but the emptiness within." The hall was crammed with students, their heads bent over their note-books, their faces deadly serious. Time and again in Japan we noticed how eagerly the Japanese of today study all forms of French culture. Sartre and Camus and others are gods, and the youth of Japan discusses existentialism with as much passion, and no doubt preciousness, as ever it was discussed with a few years ago in the Latin Quarter or in the cafés around Saint-Germain-des-Prés.

The Hiroshima express carried us through the night, past endless frozen rice-fields; by daybreak we were on the shores of the Inland Sea. It is narrow at this point and sprinkled with many small islands whose steep sides plunge sheer into the dark water. Here and there, on strips of silver sand, twisted shapes of pine-trees cluster. Huge granite rocks thrust out into the sea, forming bays where little fishing-boats hide. It is an enchanting sight. The rising sun slants its beams upon the ever changing colours of the sea.

75

76 · HONEYMOON ROUND THE WORLD

In the early afternoon the loudspeakers cried out: "Hiroshima!"
A young student had been told of our arrival and was on the
platform to meet us. With him was the Professor of French
from the university, a gaunt-faced gentleman who bowed very
low and proposed, in faultless French, to be our guide during our
visit.

The only "Western" hotel in the town is pompously entitled
Riverside House. It is a sort of wooden shanty; its beds have only
one sheet.

Life in Hiroshima, since its revival, has become infinitely
brisker and gayer than it was before the War, or so say the people
who used to know it in the old days. It has been forgotten that on
an August morning in 1945 a man sat himself down on the grey
stone steps of the Chiboyoda Bank. The day promised to be very
hot. The sirens had just sounded an air-raid alarm and hundreds of
people, proposing to take refuge in the woods thereabouts, got out
of the rickety tramways at the stop beside the bank. Hiroshima
had the usual busy air of a city in war-time.

No second warning was given for the single plane that came
over, flying at moderate height in the clear summer sky. And
then an explosion swept the town, radiating a heat so fierce that
thousands of men and women ran in flames to throw themselves
into the river. The man on the steps of the bank was instantly
turned to dust, the grey stones about him became snow-white.

From that day his silhouette has remained black upon the stone,
and every morning the people alighting from their new buses can
see, at the foot of the wall, which is still standing, the shadow of
his head.

The inhabitants of Hiroshima are now possessed of an invincible
superiority complex. Since they have been compelled to be the
guinea-pigs of atomic destruction they may as well be proud of
it. And they are. To know that other towns have suffered atrocious
bombing does not interest them. Hiroshima has become the
synonym of atomic bombardment and they are quite sure that
every language will soon contain the verb "to hiroshimise". It
flatters them to think that this dull, far-off town which must
always have been the last word in ugliness, should have become
overnight the most famous in the world. Perhaps their pride is
justified.

Once the initial panic had subsided, the survivors set to work with innate fatalism and unshakable courage to collect the fragments and build themselves huts. Men repatriated from Manchuria, Korea, and elsewhere, joined them; the bomb had destroyed a considerable number of lives but had not shaken the "Japanese Family" and its incredible stability and ramifications. Dim cousins of owners burnt alive came to claim their scraps of land. Rich speculators from Tokio often got there first and bought up properties dirt cheap which they are now selling at huge prices. Some of them have even settled in Hiroshima and, lodged in fine houses, driving in sumptuous cars, ply their despicable trade. The genuine inhabitants point them out with scorn.

For some years the municipality has engaged in an important rebuilding programme. You often see, in the new streets, poor little old shanties carted away bodily to make room for the future city. But in the reconstructed primary schools the round-faced shaven-headed children are still two for every available place.

If a few students have, in spite of their utter destitution, refused American aid, no general resentment is felt against the throwers of the bomb. The Japanese are too poor and—once again—too wholly fatalistic not to know that hatred does not pay, and instead of cursing their tragic destiny, the people have made their town a centre of hope where the words "No More Hiroshimas" have become the sincere slogan of one of the world's most wretched communities.

A few months ago a big Asiatic Buddhist Congress was held here and an oath was taken never to let such horrors occur again.

Near to the place where the members met, the largest cathedral in Asia is being built. Indeed, it is almost finished. Its architect is a German Jesuit naturalised Japanese, who was wounded by the bomb in the ruins of the University. This great church is a memorial to peace, dedicated to those who were killed by the atomic bomb and to all the victims of war. It seeks to show the spiritual rebirth of this city which the experts said would be an "atomic desert" for seventy-five years.

The financing of this project started in America but continued in Japan; the Buddhist organisations contributed largely. Many European towns have sent gifts: Cologne a fine organ, Liège a harmonium, Hamburg bells, graven with the words "Hamburg and Hiroshima, linked by a common suffering, work and pray for the peace of the world." Other martyred cities of Europe are sending stained glass.

At the foot of the cathedral stands a large, white building whose walls re-echo to the sound of scales and the discords of mixed practising. In 1947, after four years in a Japanese concentration camp, a young Belgian priest came to Hiroshima and found it in a terrifying state, both physically and spiritually. Starting with two old pianos and a violin, he opened a school of music. Four hundred young men and women promptly sought to join. Five difficult years passed. Today, if you peer through the cracked windows into the icy little white-washed rooms you may see an eager group of adolescents singing Gabriel Fauré.

In the middle of the public park, on the site of an ancient castle that now exists only on picture postcards, the people have themselves erected a tower and inscribed on its base the ultimate cry of the living and the dead: "Sleep in peace, it will never happen again." From every part of the world have come gestures of charity. An American doctor visited Hiroshima three times to direct the building, done at his own cost, of houses for the wounded and the poor. At each visit he worked himself, stripped to the waist, sawing the beams of the framework.

The streets are crowded at every hour of the day. The highly lit *Patchinko* galleries are especially full. *Patchinko* is a sort of little upright billiards table. You put in your coin and you win sweets or cigarettes, or you lose your day's wages. Fat women, their babies on their backs, congregate there, and schoolboys in their black caps and old gentlemen in striped trousers.

A third of the population is still only working from day to day. No smoke rises from the factories; the owners are dead and the newcomers too poor to refit them. The only thing is to survive, like the wretched man in the tumbledown booth who sells photographs of his horribly mutilated back, or the professor of mineralogy who was put in prison at the time of the catastrophe because he said the explosion was of an atomic nature. Now, in his little museum he arranges melted bottle-ends and tattered footwear. The bomb fell all those years ago but people still suddenly lose their hair, become anaemic, or blind, and die.

Nevertheless, in a few days the first peal of the Hamburg bells will ring out from the big cathedral of Hiroshima, voicing the tragic, ardent belief of three hundred and twenty thousand people of differing creeds in a world of peace and love.

We thanked our good friend the professor from the bottom of our hearts. He had been so kind—and so touching: his overcoat was much the worse for wear, his shoes down-at-heel, his hat faded; in all a pathetic sight. He was one of the many poor scholars that are met with all over the world, cultivated, artistic, refined in manner and taste, whose poverty is particularly affecting.

He showed us the miserable room that was his office at the university. A table covered with out-of-date reviews, a dog-eared Montaigne, a heap of grey note-books, a stained map of France held to the wall by rusty drawing-pins, wooden shelves filled with damp and dusty volumes—such is the place where the courses in French are set and corrected in the University of Hiroshima.

Not once did our friend take us to his home. No doubt he lived in one of those huts. He always came with us to our hotel at the luncheon hour, disappeared, and reappeared after we had eaten. Not once would he accept a meal. Pride, the honour of a poverty-stricken land where you never see a beggar.

The young student who came to meet us saw us off at the station. He knew a few words of French, and asked Alietfe what part of France she came from. "From Dauphiné," she told him, and he cried out, delighted: "The home of Stendhal!" Seeing our astonishment, he added: "I am a Stendhalian."

The train bore us away to Osaka.

18

A Visit
to the Marionettes

OSAKA is an important industrial town; it manufactures most of the cheap Japanese bric-à-brac that floods the world's markets and helps this overpopulated country to survive. It calls itself "the Venice of Japan" (every city that has a canal running through it is a "Venice"), but is not of itself interesting. What we had come for was the Marionette Theatre, which used to be more famous than the Kabuki and is only seen at Osaka.

Puppets originated in China and were for a long time a form of entertainment reserved exclusively for certain religious sects; the people did not enjoy them until the sixteenth century. Their performance is a dramatised ballad, written in verse of alternate five and seven syllables, recited to the music of the *samisen*, a kind of mandolin made of snake skin, which is still popular in Japan.

The hall was unusually large, full of people and very dirty. On the brightly lit stage were two men in black cowls very busy with a doll which was roughly the size of a three-year-old child. Behind it one got occasional glimpses of the puppet-master's wrinkled head. He was old—eighty-six, they said—blind and very famous. The dolls looked the same as the figures of the traditional prints— women in heavy wigs and richly coloured kimonos, men with half-shaven heads and upslanting, heavily made-up eyes.

The narrator sat cross-legged before a desk in a corner of the hall and read the ballad text in a shrill, harsh voice. The tone varied according to whether a woman was concerned or a man. He was fat and violently flushed; and threw himself about, screaming, weeping and making faces.

More men in black cowls presently appeared manipulating two puppets in authentic, ancient costume. The blind man was behind the heroine and worked her head and right arm. He was wildly applauded. The Japanese have put him in a special class; he is a "national figure". His two acolytes worked the left arm and the legs. The effect was striking; every emotion was expressed: the excitement of hope, the rigidity of fear, the tremors of anger, the shrinking of pain.

The performance was so excellent that without understanding one of the strange words that accompanied it we followed the highly dramatic action perfectly.

Two brothers were defending the conflicting interests of their overlords. Their father, witnessing their terrible quarrel, was in despair, overcome by excess of grief. One of the brothers imagined that he had been insulted by the other and prepared to commit hara-kiri. His wife pleaded with him not to do this dreadful thing. Stifling her sobs she flung herself at his feet. Curtain.

But the husband refused to listen to her. Crouched on his heels, his body stiffly erect, he remained unmoved by her entreaties; his face was sad, contemptuous, noble. The lady knelt before him; her arms, outstretched in supplication, trembled. The unhappy father was silent, for he knew what honour requires of a man.

The act of hara-kiri followed, a very moving sight. The puppet —in the raucous tones of the narrator—sang the song of his resolve; by an almost imperceptible movement, he brought the point of his dagger to his belly.

In this dramatic scene the simplicity of Japanese art reaches its highest level; every gesture was so extraordinarily controlled that the spectator hardly realised that the irreparable deed had been done until he saw the body jerk and quiver as the knife at last ripped upward. The narrator uttered the final sigh as the body collapsed.

The curtain fell on a landscape full of flowers and the figure of the father, dressed in a Buddhist robe, leaning on a stick and slowly making his way, aged, absorbed in contemplation, to some distant place of pilgrimage.

F

19

Mikimoto's Fabulous Isle

THERE were no seats for us in the electric railcar, but the moment we climbed in, a dozen people jumped to their feet, women as well as men, and signed to us to sit down. They went on talking to each other or reading their papers as though what they had done was the most natural thing imaginable. A drunkard with a snowy-white beard jostled two passengers, gave a push to a third, who did not seem to notice, and plumped himself down beside us, holding out gifts of cigarettes and tangerines. His smiles were so broad, his only front tooth so large that Aliette. burst out laughing. Everyone turned to look at us.

He then gave his most passionate attention to the case of our typewriter. Without hesitation he opened it, examined its contents, tried the carriage, hit a key, mishandling our machine in every possible way and muttering incomprehensively to himself. This extreme interest, this taste for exact observation, are what makes the Japanese the world's prize counterfeiters. A Swiss friend had been telling us how he took his wireless set to an electrician to be repaired; a valve was burnt out. He was asked to come back in three days, which he did. But the set was not ready. The electrician, apologising profusely, said that further repairs were needed and would our friend come back in a week? But again there was no set, whereupon the owner got annoyed, became insistent and, pushing his way into the workshop, found his wireless set dismantled and three workmen busy making copies of it in every detail.

So it is not surprising that a small village in the south of Japan

that specialises in clock and watch-making has been given the
name Switzerland, and that every product of its factories should
be marked "Made in Switzerland".

The drunkard had done with our typewriter. We were slowing
down anyway and coming to Ujiyamada, where we were to take
a motor coach to the Pacific Coast. In the creek of Toba is an
island which we were going to visit, where live thousands of
oysters that produce the famous cultured pearls.

Old Mikimoto's name is as well-known as the Emperor's. On the
day we visited his island he was still alive, rising ninety-seven and
remarkably active. All the newspapers burst into columns of print
if he so much as catches a cold. It was he who, at the end of the
last century, discovered a way of making oysters secrete artificial
pearls. The process is very simple and soon brought him fame and
a large fortune. Everyone knowns and admires the cultured pearl.

The virtues of publicity are well appreciated in those parts. We
were greeted at the landing-stage by one of the directors, the
usual smiling little gentleman, who led us to the foot of the hill
where a series of buildings run along by the waterside. The first
is a sort of laboratory. Behind a score or so of tables, young
women in white overalls were treating the oysters. They picked
them out of tubs, half-opened them with the aid of small pincers,
made an incision in the flesh and inserted a tiny porcelain bead.
The oysters were then closed again, put into other tubs and sent
back to the huge beds that are slung in the sea by means of floats.
Well fed, frequently cleaned, they remain in this pseudo-natural
home for five or seven years and form about the tiny bead the
nacreous substance that makes the pearl. We all know that the
pearl is a disease of the oyster; it took a Mikimoto to think up the
minute intrusion and provoke the disease artificially.

In the second building girls were collecting the pearls, sorting
them out according to size, shape, and sheen, and piercing them
with an infinitesimal drill. They were then strung into necklaces, a
stage of the proceedings that interested Aliette particularly. To
the amusement of our guide, she dipped her hands into the bowl
of pearls, picked out the largest and rolled them in her palms
with cries of pleasure.

The next performance was that of the divers. Despite the cold,
three shivering girls went into the water, each bearing a knife.

They splashed about, dived and after a minute or so came up with handfuls of oysters. They did it again and again. The director's face wore a smugly satisfied expression. The girls looked frozen. Aliette was outraged that trade should be so cruel.

Our visit did not end as we had hoped in an oyster feast; the pearl oyster is not edible. We were given something better. In a small private room a servant brought in a dozen oyster-shells on a plate, and our guide invited us to choose one each. Aliette could not make up her mind and stared at the plate for a long while.

The little man opened my shell, rummaged around and produced one small pearl. I was very disappointed. But Aliette, between excitement and anxiety, was jumping up and down on her chair. She shrieked with joy; hers were two pearls of quite fine quality.

20

Off to Korea

BACK in Tokio, Aliette began to get worried over the way her work with the dressmaking firm would turn out. In the evenings I would see her turning over the pages of fashion magazines. Drawings littered the floor of the more comfortable room another friend, Francois D . . ., had found for us in the suburbs. We slept on *tatamis* and were looked after by a charming little maid.

It seemed that all Aliette's time would be taken up. And I dislike playing the Prince Consort anyway. As it happened, however, I had the luck to meet the editor of a big daily who asked me if I would go to Korea and do a series of articles on the Korean youth. I jumped at the offer.

But even though backed by a newspaper it was not so easy to get to Korea. I had to go to the former Japanese Military Academy, now the headquarters of the USA General, and obtain a permit. Once again I found myself in the overheated passages and offices of America, alive with smart lady secretaries. A young captain received me to the jazz strains of a portable wireless. I filled up a form that would be cabled to Washington; my "political history" had to be looked into.

There was no delay. In five days I was given my permit. Yet before getting into the plane I had still to run all over Tokio chasing my correspondent's card and my identity card for the United States Armies (in duplicate in case the Chinese put me in prison) and having notes made of my religion and my blood-group, lest I should need medical care or Extreme Unction. I then had to collect my "special mission" papers and the whole of the extraordinary equipment issued to the American forces. Our little

85

maid lovingly sewed on to my sleeve the badge of "United Nations War Correspondent" and I kissed Aliette good-bye. She did not appear at all disturbed at our parting, although it was the first. "I think it is a very good thing," she explained most logically, "to be away from each other for a while. We shall be so happy when we meet again!"

At the last moment, I found I was still short of several inoculations. Somewhat encumbered by my fur boots, I rushed to the nearest military hospital and was given injections against cholera, typhus, typhoid, smallpox and influenza by a young American sergeant.

But finally I caught the train to Tatchikawa, the big American aerodrome. My clothes were stifling; I was sweating at every pore and my face was surely purple. The other passengers glanced at me with complete indifference—which was a trifle wounding.

At Tatchikawa a jeep picked me up and took me to the aerodrome. The immense waiting-room was exactly like any other of the commercial type: white-painted ceiling and walls, concealed lights, flower-pots, windows with little green curtains, engravings. In one corner was a book-stall and in another a sweet-kiosk. At the back, behind a long counter, immaculate uniformed officers strolled up and down. A large blackboard gave the schedule of flights for the night: Okinawa, Seoul, Fusan, etc.

I sat down in one of the big blue leather arm-chairs. The place was full of soldiers in battle dress, fully armed, who were smoking or reading magazines. The nasal voice of the loudspeaker never ceased. "Lieutenant Macdonald is wanted at operations office"; "Passengers for Flight 325 are requested to go to the embarkation ground". Some men rose, gathered up their kit, put out their cigarettes and vanished.

Every now and then an air-crew went by, their revolvers in their holsters, their parachutes on their backs. Negro pilots looked even blacker in their blue fur jackets. I went and ate a sandwich at the express bar where little Japanese waitresses in white blouses darted swiftly back and forth. I paid in military currency which is based on the dollar. Everywhere, even in the luxurious lavatories, were "suggestion boxes" begging you to say if the service was not satisfactory and what you suggested should be done about it. The male personnel were clean, well dressed and well fed.

"Attention! Attention! Passengers for K 16 (Seoul) please get

ready to embark." I snatched up my bag and went out into the
night. It was bitterly cold and I praised heaven for my fur-lined
clothes. The engines of a big C 14 were turning over with a roar.
A young officer, a large pink form in his hand, preceded us. He
stopped in front of the cabin and called out: "Passengers will
please come up in the order named: Colonel Whitten, Monsieur
Lapierre, Major . . ." I was much astonished at being second on
the list. Apparently all war correspondents are given the rank and
privileges of a colonel or a major in the American Army.

I took a seat as far forward as possible, just behind the cockpit.
The entire centre of the plane was taken up by packing-cases
marked in large red letters, "Human Blood. With Care". The passengers piled in as best they could, the door was closed. A huge
negro leaned against the cases and informed us in a strong Brook-
lyn accent that, "I am Sergeant Nelly. I am your steward. Our
Captain's name is Goodman and the co-pilot's Branoff. We shall
reach Seoul in four hours. We are going round by the south to
avoid the sea as much as possible. In case of a forced landing,
your Mae West is there over your heads. This is the way you put
it on." And he proceeded to give a demonstration that we followed
with the closest attention. In a deafening roar the plane shivered
and took off.

The heating apparatus was not working, and we huddled together to keep from freezing. The dim light from the ceiling was
not good enough to read by. From time to time the negro brought
us cups of hot coffee. He had been doing this job for twenty-five
months, he told me, with a broad grin, and was still not bored by
it. He dug a small, rather battered photograph out of his pocket
and showed it to me, laughing so that all his magnificent teeth
shone: "That's my fiancée."

We were flying over Nagoya. The lights of the town made
splashes of pale yellow in the misty portholes. Numbed by the
cold, I dozed off.

"Stand by! Put on your belts. We are landing at Seoul." I
glanced at my watch. It was 1.30 a.m.

The waiting-room at Seoul aerodrome was overheated and full
of soldiers of every nationality: Australians, Canadians, Greeks,
Ethiopians. They were asleep on the benches, their guns and
revolvers on their stomachs, their helmets under their heads, their
shoes covered with mud. The feel of the place was very different

from Tatchikawa; the Chinese were only thirty miles away. A jeep was waiting for me. What a thing American organisation is! The PIO (Public Information Office) knew of the arrival of every correspondent. A young Korean drove me to Seoul—at first, to my astonishment, with the headlights full on. But presently a luminous sign gave a warning, "Complete blackout for two miles", and we slowed down and crawled in the utter darkness over the Han bridge. A gigantic MP examined our papers and the car. Beyond the bridge we speeded up again and the headlights reappeared. And now we were in Seoul; we saw the first charred and broken walls. On every tree hung notices, just like those on Fifth Avenue: "No parking. Maximum speed thirty miles." An occasional lamppost cast a dreary light over the torn roadsides. We took the broad avenue that led to the Capitol which old Rhee wanted to destroy because the Japanese had built it. The car turned leftward and stopped with a screeching of tyres before a signboard: "Seoul Correspondents' Billets." I thanked my silent and impassive companion and went into a narrow room. A soldier in his shirtsleeves was asleep on a camp-bed. He awoke and, rubbing his eyes, got up, welcomed me by name mechanically and led me to the third floor. On each door is a printed notice: "The Times", Associated Press", "Daily Mail", "Agence France Presse", etc. The room I entered was lit by a single electric bulb and occupied by two sleeping men. One, who looked elderly, snored and went on snoring. The other—a gigantic fellow—rolled over on his camp-bed, opened an eye, arose and shook me by the hand.

"My name's Patrick. I'm the correspondent of the London *Observer.*"

He fetched a bottle of whisky, offered me some, knocked back a good dose himself and went to sleep again.

The room was so hot that I lay down on top of my sleeping-bag for my first night in Seoul.

21

A Front-line Feast

NEXT morning was radiantly fine. Out of the window, while I shaved I could see ruined houses and a huddle of wooden shanties and, tripping about them, a number of little girls in long pink frocks. On the horizon stretched a ridge of hills.

My first and most important duty was to call on the director of the Press Club, Major Brown. He was a tired-looking little man. A bottle of gin was produced and a full glass poured out for me. Major Brown had been here since the beginning and was responsible for the remarkable organisation of which I was already getting full benefit. "Oh!" he said. "Journalists aren't always easy to handle but they're very good chaps. You're heartily welcome. Don't forget to ask me for anything you want."

I ate my breakfast at the club cafeteria, served by excessively polite Koreans. For the small sum of forty cents they gave one coffee, porridge, bacon and eggs, orange-juice, toast, butter and jam. My room-mate came in, and I told him how amazed I was at the whole press set-up.

"You will see more of it presently," he answered; "it won't take you long to realise the immense importance that the Americans attach to keeping their people well informed. I know something about it! I was war correspondent in Indo-China. They don't like journalists in Indo-China! They scarcely give you any help. I might say that compared with these chaps they don't give you any help at all. To them a journalist is a dangerous character. Do you remember the defeat at Caobang? You had to have a disaster before the public were told a word. It's a bad policy. The French are often said not to care about the war in Indo-China. How can they when they never hear of it? Look at the Americans. They'll spend millions just to tell some fiddling little Middle West rag that

89

a GI wears fur boots! And the sort of fur they're made of! Like the public relations men in the business firms telling the customer what he's buying and what it's for."

"But there is a censorship," I put in.

"There is," he retorted, "but here it isn't the man who is told off to help you do your job who does the censoring. The two organisations are quite separate. In Indo-China there were people, Bao Dai for instance, I was never allowed to interview. And places I was never allowed to see. Here you can go anywhere. If you want to talk to Syngman Rhee or take fifty front-line photographs you may. Everything will be made easy for you. . . ."

"Yes, of course . . . but the American Army has the means of——"

He waved his hand and interrupted me: "I don't believe it's a question of means. It's the idea, the different attitude of mind. . . ."

There were few civilians in the streets of Seoul. Or rather there were very few men who did not wear some sort of queer uniform. Convoys passed ceaselessly up and down. The town was clean. The ruined houses had been patched up with boards and tarpaulins and paper, as they were in France in 1944. On the walls you saw occasional graffiti: "Welcome America."

At the liaison office of the United Nations French Battalion I made the acquaintance of a young officer who offered to introduce me next day to his unit. As I left him I ran into an elderly American major. He flung his arms round my neck. "I must hug you," he cried. "I've just had orders to go home!" I congratulated him warmly.

I got ready to start for the line in good time. It was a great day; the battalion was expecting General Juin. But my officer friend could not find his chauffeur. That gentleman turned up at last, half an hour late. "You see, mon Lieutenant," he said, "my Korean girl friend wouldn't let me go. They don't often get a Frenchman and, well, the Yanks . . ."

We left Seoul by a beaten-earth road thick with dust. The sky was a deep blue. We crossed little crests and valleys chequered with frozen rice-fields. A rare civilian trudged by, his bundle on his back. Before their wooden huts, women in long dresses bustled about their cooking, their saucepans shining in the sun. Children squatted beside shoe-shine outfits and signed to us to stop. Lorries full of soldiers covered us with thick clouds of dust. Crouching between a case of shells and the jeep's heating unit, I was far from happy; it was the first time I had ever visited a battle-line. The chauffeur, an excellent driver who had seen all the wars, hummed to himself or chattered of the little 4-hp car that was waiting for him when he got back home to France. When we heard a shell-burst, he would remark: "Eh! That's one for the English, that's one for the Yanks."

To be on the safe side I put on my helmet and sat well back. The car was skidding wildly over the ruts left by a convoy of British tanks that had just gone by. A signboard: The Thirty-Eighth Parallel—the end of the civilian's world.

Notices hung from the blasted trees announcing a near-by first-aid post, a car-park, or a battery. The earth was red, stony, grim. Yet it was hard to realise that this was a war zone. It was my officer friend who reminded me. "We are now within range of the Chinese guns."

We turned off to the left and made for the line. A notice warned us that tin hats and bullet-proof waistcoats must be worn. "Oh! those Yanks!" said our chauffeur, "they're always the same," and instead of putting on his helmet he unbuttoned his tunic because he felt too hot.

Two shells fell spluttering on the road five hundred yards ahead. At this point, a couple of days ago, "three Englishmen copped it. . . ." We crossed a railway and a pipe-line running along-side it and gleaming in the sunlight. What a target for enemy air-craft. A sharp bend, and I noticed a frozen rice-field surrounded by a palisade. "That," the chauffeur told us without being asked, "is an ice-hockey rink the Canadians fixed up."

A moment later the Tricolour was before us flying from a white flag-staff. At the foot was a placard: "French Battalion of the UNO. Second to none." We were some five hundred yards from the Chinese, and the dull sounds of explosions recurred at regular intervals.

A captain came to meet us and I was introduced without delay. He was tall and smiling and spoke with a faint Slav accent. "Would you like to see the Chinese positions?" "Yes, with pleasure."

Preceded by a huge alsatian he had secretly brought out from

France, we climbed the first ridge, descended into a hollow where men were busy with their mortars, and then climbed up a second ridge. The Chinese lines were perfectly clear.

I inquired innocently: "Do you think they can see us?" "Of course! With a field-glass they can make out every line on your face!" I ducked down a little.

Suddenly there was a whistling, tearing noise. A dozen American planes turned in the sunshine and dived about three hundred yards ahead of us, dropping out round black objects that exploded with a dull thud. "Napalm," my companion murmured. The slopes opposite caught fire; the planes climbed at full speed and immediately dived again. It was most impressive. The whistling noises followed by the dull explosions went on for quite a while. Meantime, shells from the enemy mortars were falling on our lines.

"The Chinese," the captain explained, "are so deeply dug in that this sort of thing hardly affects them. It is almost impossible to locate their batteries. The guns are underground. They come up, fire a few rounds and disappear before we have time to answer effectively."

The valley was utterly deserted; the peaks were grey and bare, wretched-looking even in the splendid winter sunshine. I was stifling inside my bullet-proof waistcoat.

The dog crawled in front of us, looking round at intervals to make sure that his master was following. We reached a prefabricated blockhouse; bunkers and everything are sent out from America and only need assembling. Smoke was coming out of a chimney. How was it that the Chinese did not pound such a place to atoms with the greatest ease?

"Have an aperitif?" asks the chaplain. Every morning he went up to the front lines, bringing the men sweets and reading-matter. A lot of young officers were about, some of them wearing the Croix de Guerre; there had been an investiture that morning. I had taken off my helmet and bullet-proof waistcoat and felt very comfortable in this big, shadowy den. Cookhouse boys brought in bottles of wine, and the colonel signed to us to start our meal. He was a small man with an intelligent, distinguished face. All the officers were there except those kept in the line by the Chinese shelling.

"Oh! you needn't worry. We always get a few about luncheon-time."

The explosions made our glasses rattle.

"By the way," asked the little lieutenant, stroking his little moustache. "Have they told you about Anatole?" I shook my head and he went on: "Anatole is a Chinese machine-gunner just opposite my section. You wouldn't believe what a good chap he is! He knows exactly where we are but he always misses us on purpose. And he never keeps it up too long. We don't want him replaced by some nasty, wicked fellow if we kill him. So we never shoot back. . . ."

We sat down to a positive feast:

> *Pâté en croûte*
> *Filets de poisson sauce tomate*
> *Rôti de veau pommes frites*
> *Gazelle braisée aux haricots verts*
> *Salade, fromage*
> *Gâteau de chocolat*
> *Café, liqueurs*

All that and a delicious vin rosé too. I asked my neighbour how they got hold of the gazelle. He put on a mysterious air and whispered that one of the captains had been specially appointed to bag some game whenever the cook required it.

The telephone rang.

"Doctor! They've just picked up two corpses in the rice-fields. You're wanted in the Infirmary."

The doctor, a big fellow with curly hair, went out, bare-headed. The meal proceeded. Presently he came back. We all looked at him inquiringly.

"Roger and Pierre. Burst of tommy-gun fire in the lungs. Weren't wearing their waistcoats."

The doctor sat down. My neighbour turned to him:

"No one in the battalion ever wears a waistcoat."

"A great mistake. You see what happens . . ."

"We aren't Americans. We're making war!"

"That's nothing to do with it. You can make war and still protect yourself as much as possible."

"Can't be done," said the lieutenant. "Bad for morale."

"For morale?"

"Yes. You see—if I cover my belly and my chest I shall be afraid my arms will get hurt. And if my arms are safe, I shall be afraid for my legs. So it's better to chance the lot——"

A terrific clatter invaded the mess. We all jumped to our feet: "It's Alphonse! It's Alphonse!"

A helicopter flew up the valley that opened just behind the line. A second followed it, a third, then another and another. Clouds of dust covered their landing. Out of one of them stepped Juin and Clark, General Allard and General Taylor, the C-in-C of the South Korean armies. They walked forward and a small company of men presented arms. From afar came the intermittent clacking of machine-guns; the sky was absolutely blue. Juin reviewed the men, then climbed up the hill with the colonel to look at the Chinese front. The others stayed below; there was no need to attract too much attention. Coming down the Marshal slipped on a stone and lost his balance. In the mess he and his escort gathered round the champagne bottles and an enormous cream cake. The officers of the battalion clustered round them. A few foreign correspondents were there also.

The Marshal spoke in a somewhat gruff voice. "I am happy," he began, "to see Frenchmen who have had the courage to come so far to show our friends France's high qualities. The cause of the free world . . ."

A proper oration, clinking of glasses, other speeches returning thanks, noise of bursting shells. Juin grasped the hands held out to him with his left hand. General Clark smiled amiably. He was so tall that he had to keep his head bent to avoid the beams that supported the sandbag ceiling. He had style.

The visit was short. Once again the rotors of the helicopters started to revolve. The travellers climbed in and the machines glided off down the valley as fast as they could go, almost at ground level.

Near sunset an American officer came to fetch me in a jeep and took me to the aerodrome of the 2nd Division. From there I could get back to Seoul; I had been invited to follow Marshal Juin the next day on his tour of inspection of the training centres of the South Korean Army.

My companion was a big, fair chap. He came from Texas. His shoes were exquisitely polished.

"Oh! you Frenchmen! You do get around! Do you know that to be invited to eat in your battalion's mess is a rare privilege?"

I liked the man for having said such a nice thing and so sincerely, so spontaneously. What a pity the men of whom he spoke like that should themselves show so much less kindliness. "Americans! They don't know how to make war. . . ."

At the 2nd Division aerodrome I was told that two planes had just been shot down and that I should have to wait a bit. On the runway reconnaissance planes were landing and taking off in quick succession. Their pilots jumped out, unloaded their cameras and started again instantly.

"The flak is pretty bad today," said a little airman with a scarred face, "but visibility is so good I can't bear to waste it." He adjusted his parachute and was gone.

Every human cog in the American war-machine did his job as though it were sport; every man was clean, smiling, civil-spoken and without bitterness. "We'd rather be elsewhere of course but since we're here we must get on with it as well as we can."

The men I could see tapping now at their typewriters in their big tent had been torn by force from the peaceful life they had been leading in some corner of California or Kansas. They had been transplanted to the ends of the earth for reasons they could scarcely understand. Their *job* had suddenly become another *job*, which they carried out as conscientiously as they had carried out their former one, with the same unaltering smile which was a very pleasant thing to see in a land where men were dying every day. They knew of course that everything was being done to protect them and that millions were being expended to save their lives. A man wounded in the front line would be in hospital in under twenty minutes, and surgeons would move about him night and day. Every pilot carried a transmitter that allowed him, if he were shot down, to give his position and helicopters would then go, under enemy fire if necessary, to bring him in.

A Piper-Cub landed and stopped before the tents. "The passenger for Seoul!" shouted a colonel from the cabin. "Quick! I'm in a hurry."

I jumped into the plane and we raced up the runway. The ricefields looked like monster panes of glass shining in the low sun. A chain of mountains loomed up, misty in the fading light. We flew over great rocky spaces, flanked by sharp peaks and spurs that gleamed white and naked. Villages, earth-coloured, scarcely distinguishable from the soil, were just visible at times, their rounded roofs seeming no more than tiny bubbles.

A white road and a string of lorries that blotted out the landscape in an impenetrable pall of dust; a car-park, each car exactly in line; a petrol-tank, a field hospital . . . and at last Seoul, a jumble of little boxes set among dark hills. The pilot put me down and started off again instantly.

8. KOREA: Children in the grounds of a ruined temple, near Seoul

9. KOREA: Young and old alike await the daily distribution of food

10. MACAO: Beyond the barrier lies Communist China

11. HONG-KONG: A row of houses in the New Territories

22

Touring Korea with Marshal Juin

DAYBREAK and a thin, icy wind. I went to the aerodrome and drank a cup of coffee with the chief pilot. He was a
negro; the cold had turned his face yellow.

A large, camouflaged Chevrolet rolled up, and the C-in-C of
the South Korean Army alighted, a man of about thirty, his
revolver stuck in his belt. He smiled at us. After him in a string of
cars appeared Juin and Clark, a French General and three
colonels, the Commander of the 8th Army, other officers, the
military attaché, the French Ambassador to Tokio, etc. Two
planes were waiting. The VIPs climbed into the first, the others
and I into the second. A fair-haired young officer distributed sandwiches and mugs of hot coffee. We were flying through soft grey
cloud at a high altitude. I wondered aloud—if there was a fighter
escort?

"No," they told me. "But the position of the two planes is
always known. If a single Chinaman crossed the line we would
have an escort before he got within range."

We landed at Chwanju; a South Korean guard of honour presented arms; and suddenly—the *Marseillaise*! I was deeply moved
to hear it played by a little military school band, lost in this god-
forsaken corner of the earth.

We all climbed into jeeps and started quickly on our tour of the
training centre, one of those big establishments where the Americans are putting into practice their system for producing efficient
soldiers in record time. First room: a short lecture by a young
American officer explaining the object of the centre and the

G   97

results obtained. We then entered a vast hall where there were only girls squatting on the floor, and another where there were only boys. A man stood before the blackboard talking in a shrill voice. The pupils listened in complete silence, their arms folded, their shaven heads nodding gravely. A guttural order and they all rose, got themselves rifles and sat down again cross-legged, their weapons on the ground before them. The Korean professor called out the name of each part of the gun, and the pupils repeated it, taking hold of the part in question.

"The striker!" shouted the man.

"The striker!" echoed the boys in chorus.

We went to the dormitories, all scrupulously clean and tidy, and even into the kitchens where charts told one, in English and Korean, the number of calories in every meal. This school, the officer in charge told me in English, is a replica of a school of telecommunication established in Oklahoma. "We use the same methods and get the same results."

The lesson-books were duplicated copies of a special American manual. In the classrooms the walls were covered with diagrams and every room contained a model. One of these demonstrated the radio-telephone connexions employed by different units in the field. In one corner was a little doll fishing in a pond. General Clark laughed out loud and pointed out the doll to the Marshal: "Look, Marshal. There's Mr Clark trying to catch his fish." Juin gave a faint smile.

Schools of artillery, of tanks, of engineering. The factory which the Americans had built was working to capacity and was turning out a technician fully trained in two or three weeks. In the special little aerodrome, light planes were taking off and landing incessantly; a notice informed us in big red letters that the percentage of accidents was smaller than in most United States training schools. The men were very young. You are an officer at twenty in the Korean Army. Those visitors who had been in Indo-China ought to have been able to learn a lot here, yet I heard two French colonels saying to each other:

"There's nothing new in all this. We've been doing the same for years in Viet-Nam." "Of course! Though the position there is a bit different. The Americans take a man and teach him everything from how to use soap to working Radar. We couldn't do that with Viet-Namese."

The troops presented arms, the band struck up and we were off again. The VIPs' plane shone in the sun. Then we were over the sea, at the southernmost point of Korea. The waves were very green, stained with dark patches and with black. Whitish foam curled at the water's edge, streaked with black seaweed. Tiny islets that showed no sign of life were followed abruptly by the rounded, snowy hills of the island we were about to visit. The sky had become grey, and the flat coast-line was wrapped in a transparent veil of mist. The pilot circled a rock, lost height, circled round the island again and again to get into line with the long grassy track that ran straight to the sea. He came down, swept by a line of waiting jeeps, almost grazed the ground and was once more high over the sea. What was going on? The other plane had landed without mishap. The manœuvre started all over again. It seemed endless and we looked at one another anxiously. Boom! the wheels had struck the ground. Up we went again and for the third time circled the rock. I was sweating. We came down at a great speed. Boom-boom, the plane bounced over the uneven ground. The green light that should have signalled the dropping of the undercarriage never appeared.

We jumped into a jeep driven by a plump American colonel with grizzled hair. "Life is pleasant here," he said. "The men are all working well and I've got a nice little Korean girl friend who cooks beautifully." He laughed and added: "You'll see what a first-rate job we're doing."

The road climbed up the hill between stretches of rough stone and steep, sharp slopes. One had to stare and stare before one could make out that hundreds of men were exercising there. Wonderfully camouflaged, they crawled forward and threw their grenades. Little dust-clouds arose. An officer snapped out an order and the men jumped out of the scrub.

On the hill-top was a flat plateau on which a platform had been set up. We went there to watch the "battle course". It was highly realistic. The plateau was full of holes and barbed wire and other obstacles. Below the platform crouched the machine-gunners; on it an officer shouted his orders through a megaphone. All about him men were hurling grenades, the machine-guns searing the ground with trails of bullets. A group of men broke out of a small coppice, flung themselves on their bellies and began to crawl forward. The clatter of machine-guns increased, the grenades fell like rain, the recruits crawled on, wriggling under the barbed wire. Wherever a man failed to keep down, a burst of fire went over his head, the officer shouted into his megaphone, the shooting stopped and the man was beaten with a cudgel by the young officers. Farther off, bayonet practice was proceeding with the usual dummies and fierce yells.

On my way down to the aerodrome, I caught sight of a prison-camp. In their barbed-wire enclosures the Chinese prisoners, warmly clad in American uniforms, were smoking cigarettes. "They're not a bit pleased," our colonel said. "Their GI guards have been taken off and Koreans put on. Please do not take any photographs. Strict orders."

Our time-table was punctual to the minute: the visit was over. Marshal Juin, weighed down by the fur boots he had been lent, climbed with some difficulty into his plane. A few moments later we were at Fusan. General Clark's "personal" Constellation was ready to take the VIPs back to Tokio. A guard of honour presented arms. Juin gave a slack left hand to the people about him. Clark walked up and down, dignified and benevolent. To my amazement he strolled over to me and said, "I know someone who knows your wife."

I could not help thinking that he must have been mistaken and was muddling me up with some more important person. But no. Seeing my bewilderment, he added, "Surely your wife met my friend Verdier, the president of the 'City of Paris' in San Francisco?" and of course it was at the 'City of Paris' that Aliette sold ties! Not very long after, the C-in-C sent us a charming invitation to cocktails at his house.

The Constellation took off. I wondered how the Marshal could stand up, apparently without fatigue, to such a life. He had done over fifty hours' flying, had visited the Indo-Chinese front and had now spent two exhausting days in Korea—all in a week.

An hour later I was back at Seoul. At the Press Club the spotty little sergeant on duty handed me a long letter from Aliette. I lay down on my sleeping-bag to read it.

23

Aliette as a Professor

"You know how eager I was to come to Japan and see the women in kimonos who receive their guests so beautifully and arrange flowers and lead a refined, dignified life. I believed in the legend and imagined every Japanese woman to be a Madame Butterfly.

"Well my poor dear! The more I see of them the more certain I am that my grand ideals were all fairy-tales. They are exactly like us, these women! You saw them in the street dressed like Europeans and very badly at that. And you saw how only one in ten wears a kimono. They all want to live what they call the modern life and get work at any price. I saw Mrs Sogawa this morning and asked her why they were so keen to destroy the charm of Japanese life. She nearly lost her temper with me.

" 'Oh! you foreigners! You think the old ways and the background lovely, don't you? You want exotic charm and you're disappointed when you don't find it! Do you know what a Japanese woman is *really* like? She is a slave and always has been. First she has to serve her mother—it's a disgrace to have girl children—and then her husband. And she can't choose her husband; he is chosen for her and neglects her most of the time. She never goes out with him except on some family occasion. If she does, she must walk three paces behind him. The men drink a lot and spend their money, if they have any, with the geishas, who are specially trained to please them, who dance and sing and recite poetry and do everything to anticipate their slightest whims. They are not at all shy, so our husbands have much more fun with them than with us. We are accustomed to serve and to be ill-treated; they take

full advantage of that but they find us dull. That's why we want
to be free, to work, to have lives of our own.
"'You ask why we want to give up the kimono? Because it is
an out-worn symbol and most unpractical. The *obi* and the sleeves
get in the way of the typewriter. We can't jump into motor-buses
in a tight skirt that opens down the front. The *getas* make a horrid
clatter on the pavements. Oh! no, no! All that's over. We are going
to have something to say for ourselves now!'
"Mr Imaida, the editor of *Soen*, quite without meaning to, confirmed all this. He is going to France presently, and when I asked
him if his wife was going too he looked at me as if I were out of
my senses. 'Of course not! My wife stays at home. She is not
interested in what I do and I don't see much of her. In the evenings, after my work, I go out with friends and seldom get back
before midnight!' •
"What do you think of that for married life? Lovely, isn't
it?
"Yesterday I gave my first lesson at the dress-making school.
They made me drink vast quantities of green tea and then took
me to the lecture-hall. The place was absolutely chock-full. Just
think! More than two thousand pupils! I must say that for a
moment or two I was rather shaken. I stared at those little round
faces and those little sloping eyes looking up at me—all so surprised and pleased. They had told me how to say 'How d'you do'
in Japanese, so I took a good grip on myself and spoke the magic
words and the reaction was quite all right. It seemed to delight
them and put them at their ease. I told them about fashion and
how it was a question of taste and fancy. You may think this over-
simple, but to the girls it was a revelation. Their clothes haven't
altered for generations. I tried to explain the difference between
a national costume that is in a tradition and invariable, and
European fashions that change all the time, pick up ideas here,
there and everywhere, and depend on hundreds of different
factors, economic, artistic, social.
"So the Japanese are wrong to think that it is enough to put on
a skirt and a pullover to be in the latest Paris fashion. You must
know how to put them on, what materials to choose, what colours
and what accessories to wear with them. They had never dreamed
of such things. Talking to them and answering their questions I
realised that they had no notion whatsoever of chic. For instance,

they have never worn jewellery of any kind and whatever they do wear is somehow based on tradition. It appears that the way a married woman does her hair is different from the way a girl does hers and that they have special clothes for every special ceremony. Not much chance for individual inspiration! I drew plenty of drawings for them on the blackboard to show how we get our ideas from Ancient Greek draperies, from the Second Empire and so on. Just to show them how fancy and caprice influence fashion I told them the story of Louis the Fourteenth's red heels which made them laugh a lot!

"Going out you would have thought I was the greatest film-star who ever lived! I was so crushed by girls wanting autographs that, being against the wall, I got my back covered with white plaster and the director had to restore order. And, to crown it all, I had, as you know, to repeat my lecture twice. The pupils couldn't all get into the hall. I had six thousand of them that one day.

"By 8 o'clock I was worn out. I asked the director if it wouldn't be simpler for the lecture to be read out directly in Japanese. (The interpreter can't translate easily as I go along. I have to give her my piece three days beforehand so that she can get it well into her head.) He seemed flabbergasted. 'But we can't do that!' he cried. 'It's you! It's you they want! They don't miss your least little movement, your smallest change of expression!' I felt I was some strange sort of beast in a zoo!

"This evening I must prepare my next two lectures. One will be on Haute Couture in Paris, how it is organised, who are the great dressmakers, and what the latest collections are like. In the second I shall compare French and American clothes. The Japanese don't know which to copy. They want to dress like Westerners but so far they have only the wives of American officers to go by—not much of a standard! Since all the Americans do is to transpose the Dior and Fath models, it seems to me more logical to take the Japanese straight to Paris and get them to alter the models directly to suit themselves.

"I am at it all day long. My collection, which I have to see to as well, as you know, is taking more and more of my time. I and Mrs Yoda have chosen the most ravishing Japanese materials. One could do marvels with them. There are all sorts of silks printed in delicate colours that would make the most sensational after-noon dresses. I picked out some Nagoya *obis*—white silk with small black and red and gold designs—for evening coatees, and have even thought of using them for evening shoes. And I found some striped cottons, *youkata* and *tozen* for beach-frocks and slacks. Mrs Yoda seemed delighted.

"But the mannequins are my chief worry. I saw about forty little Japanese and only four or five were any good. The others were all too big in the hips or too fat in the legs or too flat-chested. I made a most careful choice, and Mrs Yoda kept on saying 'Yes'. Yet this morning when I came to the fitting, I found my dress on one of the 'horrors'! I was absolutely furious. Why say 'yes' when you mean 'no'? What is the good of my being here? Needless to say the dress looked like nothing on the awful girl. And they are working up a fantastic amount of publicity round my name. I am a tool for them to use as they like; they even put words into my mouth that I have never spoken! And all this with a smile that is beginning to get considerably on my nerves!

"Just think! A man came to see me at the shop the other day and said: 'Lapierre San, I am a maker of Basque berets. I would like to take photographs of a mannequin wearing a beret the wrong way and of you wearing it right—the way of the Great French Fashion Expert.'

"I was horrified. I told him I loathed Basque berets, that they were not smart, only convenient, and that you wore them any way you fancied. In other words I refused to play his little game.

"This morning. Of course I can't understand a word they say, and my interpreter—who is a poor little thing and trots after me like a dog and is exploited by everybody—tells me that they often forbid her to translate some of their remarks. Anyway, this morning I was taken off in a car, I wasn't told where, and there in the studio was the man and the berets and the photographer! I was beside myself with rage. That's your Japanese with his polite smile and his 'Yes' putting you in the most impossible situations! I am beginning to realise that Mrs Yoda, underneath her sweet manner, proposes to do exactly as she pleases, and I am there for her private and particular advantage. I feel I am caught in a yellow wasps' nest. All the same I am working very hard to make the collection a success.

"Mr Yoda asked me to go with him to direct the photographing of some of the dresses for a magazine. I went. I wish you had

seen the place! First of all none of the frocks was pressed (isn't it
odd? The Japanese are supposed to be so neat!) and I refused to
have them taken in that state. But the appointment had been
fixed, the photographers were ready, the mannequins waiting. I
was faced once again with an accomplished fact. My indignant
protests did not stop them bundling the dresses pell-mell into the
car. Off we went through Tokio looking for places that would
make the best settings. This, naturally, took some time. The others
thought it quite unnecessary and got impatient; they wanted to
take fifteen dresses in one afternoon, which couldn't of course be
done if you wanted proper results. But I was so disgusted I let
them carry on. The cameramen had no taste whatsoever and were
perfectly content to take any pose against any background. It
seemed to me that I was watching real sabotage and the thought
that my name would be put to these abominations made me sick.
These constant fights are very exhausting; the dresses might have
looked delightful if nicely presented. You can imagine how depressing it was: to take a lot of trouble, to try and try to get a
decent effect and to find yourself up against people who just don't
care and are perfectly satisfied with themselves! And I am supposed to be teaching them how we work in Europe! Whatever I
say, they answer 'Yes' and do the opposite.

"Two days later one of the magazine's staff brought me the
photos. I chose the least bad, and he asked me to make him a lay-
out. I did that and put up a few ideas that he seemed to like very
much. He invited me to dinner. He knows French and doesn't
often get an opportunity of speaking it so this was his chance.

"I heard nothing more about the photographs except that Mr
Yoda was to use them for the programme of the collection. More
stupidity! No need to go to the Dress Show, just buy the programme! I said nothing; I knew the answer beforehand.

"But I was still to have a world of trouble with those pictures!
Mr Imaida, the editor of *Soen*, rang me and told me he had just
learnt they were to appear in a rival magazine. He was furious
and asked me if I knew anything about it, which was logical
enough since our contract stipulates that *Soen* should have the
exclusive photographic rights. I had never suspected Mr Yoda!
All he wants is to get as much publicity as he can for himself and
to swindle everybody!

"So I was in a nice pickle! There was every chance of Yoda losing me half the money of my contract. I rushed off to the magazine to prevent them publishing the photographs. I saw the man who invited me to dinner and told him how things stood. He seemed astonished, sorry even, swore that he knew nothing of my contract with *Soen* and promised not to publish anything. I went off and telephoned Mr Imaida to put his mind at rest. All was well.

"I thought the business was over and done with, but suddenly I got another call from *Soen*. Mr Imaida, foaming at the mouth, informed me that a printer friend had told him the photographs were in hand and about to appear. He was mad with rage; if those pictures were to be published the contract would be broken and I should not get a ha'penny. A catastrophe, the rest of our tour in danger. . . .

"I jumped into a taxi. My interpreter was miserably ashamed of the way her countrymen were behaving. 'Ah!' she sighed, 'Japanese are often like that. They're cunning, they like to cheat. I know! I'm a woman! I'm never properly paid. And I daren't complain. Japanese etiquette insists that you must always accept what is offered. They ask me out to luncheon, or to dinner, just so that I can say nothing about money . . . .'

"As for me, I was quite determined. You know me: I am not exactly a business woman but I knew the game would have to be played, this time, very cautiously.

"At the magazine office, whom should I find? Yoda! and rather staggered at seeing me! I asked for the manager and was taken into his office and given tea. He called in the editor and for about an hour we palavered without cease. But they would not give in. I explained that I had been promised the photographs would not appear and that the promise had been broken. 'We have the photographs and we shall keep them,' they said.

"I asked them how they would feel if such a trick were played on them. Their answer was a very peculiar smile. Otherwise they remained wholly impassive, repeating that it was too late, that nothing could be done. I was getting angrier and angrier. At last my little interpreter came out with a few words that were definitely helpful to me:

"'Mme Lapierre is a foreigner. You are losing face by acting as you do.'

"The two men flushed scarlet. They let go of the photographs, rose and bowed.

" 'But wait a minute,' I said. 'I'm not going out of this office without a signed paper confirming what you say.'

"And that was a good stroke too. Do you know that they started arguing again? It was perfectly clear that they still had no intention of keeping their word.

"Eventually, however, the manager wrote his piece and signed it and my interpreter, reading it out to me, gave me a look to say: 'This time it's all right. More bows, more salutations. The manager ended the session with this astounding remark: 'We're honest because you are a foreigner. Otherwise . . .'

"These are the epic moments your spouse has been enjoying with the Nippon business men. Actually I am not sorry to have had the experience. It has taught me much more about the Japanese than I could ever have learned meeting them socially. There they are, seeming as natural as possible! You know how wildly enthusiastic I was at first over the fastidiousness of the Japanese soul. I remember being very shocked when Mrs —— said once: 'Don't be in a hurry. Wait till you've lived with them. . . .' However refined and cultured they may be, they are rogues in business matters.

"I forgot to tell you that I have been going regularly to the *Soen* offices—where they are, on the contrary, extremely correct— to see the men and women editors who wanted my advice. I have helped them to choose photographs, explained to them how models should be posed, given them ideas for their layouts. I didn't know that all the fashion papers were linked with dress-making schools; they illustrate, as it were, the work done in the classes. In my establishment the editorial section has a building to itself and the women sub-editors are all old pupils of the school who have specialised in some particular line. Every one of them is nice, full of good will and ready to learn. Unfortunately they have no taste. It is not their fault, it's their upbringing and their surroundings. The school sends professors to Paris every year to learn dressmaking and to get to understand our ways. Personally I think that's nonsense as the conditions in Japan are totally different from ours.

"These schools are so important that the Dress Show of my

collection will be held at the *Tokio-Kaikan* (one of the biggest hotels, as you know, of the city), and almost entirely for the benefit of the school pupils. Isn't it comic to think that it's not the great ladies who are concerned with these things but the little working girls?

"I have at last made the acquaintance of the eminent critic A——, whom Mr Imaida was so anxious for me to meet. He gave me rather a shock. He's a little man (so-called!) with long permanently waved hair; a lock of it droops coquettishly over his brow. He wears a blouse affair with an Eton collar and corduroy trousers so as to give himself, I presume, an artistic air. The effect is disagreeably ambiguous. Moreover he is quite filthily dirty. Since I am living in Japanese style we dined as usual at the Shimbashi restaurant and bowed and scraped before kneeling down to eat. By great good luck I was given a charming interpreter, a professor of literature who specialises in Montaigne. He made it a little easier. My other companion didn't inspire me in the least; he was so ugly and disgusting I hardly dared look at him.

"The conversation got going, nevertheless, with a stenographer to take down our slightest word. It is to be reproduced in *Soen*. I began by asking him what was the idea of this meeting, and he replied that the Japanese greatly enjoy hearing other people's opinions, even when the other people were only the common herd, that they are deeply interested in the new study and discussion groups since, having lived so far under the feudal system, very few people have ever been able to express an opinion at all. Also the Japanese have no self-confidence and so feel a great admiration for anyone who can express himself clearly and firmly. I told him how disappointed I was to find that his countrymen were slavish imitators and did not attempt creative work. In women's fashions this characteristic was so marked that it was positively ridiculous.

" 'But of course,' he answered, 'even our Art, which you admire so much, comes from Chinese Art.'

"We managed to agree, finally, that a common love of discussion and criticism made a link between Japan and France. . . ."

24

The Sufferings of the Young in Korea

THE young Koreans I had seen so far, spirited, soldierly, disciplined, brave, gave one hope for this unhappy country. But I wanted to see those other young people, the ones who seem the most wretched and unfortunate in the world.

For this reason, as soon as I got back to Seoul, I called on an American officer, the Commandant of the Korean Social Welfare system. He was smallish and was wearing tortoiseshell glasses. "Your work interests me profoundly," I told him, "but what interests me most are the problems you have to face among the young."

His answer was straightforward: "I won't try to gild the pill. What do you want to see? The atrocious, the average or the best?"

"I'd like to see the lot, sir," I assured him, and he put on his furred coat and we got into a jeep.

A big half-ruined barrack of a house with a bare little garden in front was the first orphanage we came to. The door, riddled by splinters, was opened by an elderly woman in a blouse that had once been white. She grinned at the Commandant, who gave her his hand. She bowed, and kissed it. We entered an icy room. It presented a shattering sight! On a dozen pallet-beds were as many skeleton children. One of them got up and tried to warm his fleshless body by a dying brazier. He looked at us with his glassy eyes but did not speak. The misery of these children is absolutely silent. We went into other rooms: swollen stomachs, huge, deformed knees, hollow faces . . . and not a complaint, not a tear. One wondered if they were too weak to cry.

109

"There are thousands of them like this," the Commandant said. "You've no idea of the immensity of our task. We do all we can but as often as not the food and articles that we supply are resold in the black market and the children continue to die. The nurses and all the Korean people who help in our organisation do it out of charity and have practically nothing to live on."

We drove over the Han bridge, which I had crossed the other night in the pitch darkness. The river was broad and muddy. On the other side of it a crowd had gathered in a narrow alley, sealed off by three MPs.

"There used," said the Commandant, "to be over one million two hundred thousand people in Seoul. There are now about seven hundred and fifty thousand left, and many others want to come back. We have to stop them. The business of provisioning is too complicated, and if the town had to be evacuated again it would be too difficult. We have also to examine every person who comes in and goes out, for fear of North Korean spies."

We left the road and dived into a ravine which led to a further row of huts. Strung between them were washing-lines and their scraps of linen.

"This is a settlement of North Korean refugees who fled south at the time of the invasion and couldn't get back."

A group of tattered urchins surrounded us, watching us with deep mistrust. The families each occupy a corner of the hovels and fix it as they feel inclined. Through a half-open door I saw a room of barely four metres square whose walls were covered with newspaper. The floor, as in Japanese houses, was raised, and on a heap of rags six people were lying. They stiffened and stared at us fixedly. To the left of the door, beneath a hood made out of old tins, was the kitchen, dug low into the ground. The fireplace was right under the hut. This is the famous means of warming by radiating heat that Western architects have just discovered and which has been current in Korea for two thousand years.

A small boy in a coat much too long for him, his skull covered with big sores, chanced it and came out to meet us, a thin hand outstretched. Through our interpreter I asked him: "What will you do when you grow up?" "Be a soldier," he answered nonchalantly. "Why?" "To kill Communists." "Why do you want to kill Communists?"

The boy swung away, turned his head and gave me a hard look

full of hatred. "None of your business!" and ran back into the hut from which his father and mother had been watching him with expressionless faces.

But this brutal frankness is better than the corruption of the children in the Seoul byways, offering American soldiers women or plundering any jeep that pauses for more than a minute. The prisons are full of such unfortunates, spoiled and degraded by poverty and war. Poor people. . . . The pure old Korean traditions used to be handed on from father to son within the rigid compass of the family. There is no one now to receive or to transmit them. The young men are scattered to the four corners of the land, the front, the training centres, the schools—or in the towns where they practise every illicit trade and frequently end up in one of the prisons we were about to visit.

We drove through a maze of streets, past the burnt skeletons of houses, until we came to a group of twisted tree-trunks and a large blackened building: "Reformatory for Juvenile Delinquents." In a big hall a man in khaki, bobbing and bowing profusely, took an enormous key and opened the doors of the cells that lined a long, sinister-looking corridor. In each cell was a group of children huddled together barefoot (their shoes were outside in the corridor) and with only one blanket between the lot of them. They seemed to be shivering with cold.

"You over there, chewing gum, what did you do?"

"I stole wood," the boy answered humbly. "My mother hadn't any to cook the rice."

"And you on the left in the soldier's cap, why are you here?"

"I used to take the soldiers to a woman's house. They gave me food there."

They all looked so wretched, so docile. This was the place they were brought to when first caught. The police would then look up their records and, after a couple of days, bring them before the magistrates to decide whether they were to be sent back to their parents—if any—or to some orphanage or some religious institution that will look after them as best it can, or finally to a reformatory or—if their minds are disordered—an asylum. In every case the prospect was tragic enough.

I said good-bye to the Commandant and continued my tour of Seoul's miseries with Kim, the Korean interpreter. Directly we were alone, Kim turned to me, and looking at me intently said:

"Listen . . . I have been wanting to ask you something for a long time. Do you know anything about the business in France they call, I believe, the *Chevallier* Case? Have you any private information? What do you feel about it yourself?"

I told him I had vaguely read of the case in the newspapers but didn't know any details.

"Yes," he went on, speaking very slowly as though weighing every word. "But don't you think it is very wrong to have acquitted the woman? It is the justification of a criminal act and will alarm every husband in the world. My own wife says to me now: 'Kim, you ought to have married a Frenchwoman.' In Korea the woman would have been executed!"

Between a row of leprous houses, from which issued raucous sounds of jazz, and a narrow lane of broken walls, crowded with ragged children and poor women terrifically made-up, stood a grand shop, all glass and brilliance, worthy of Fifth Avenue, the American Army's Store. By the door, two negro MPs were regulating the stream of soldiers in battle dress, their pockets full of chocolates and cigarettes and shaving-cream.

The stretch of pavement, hemmed in by jeeps, that runs alongside the shop is a civilian's no-man's-land. Children drift here also, and from time to time a Korean policeman pounces upon one of them who has been making obscene signs at some idle GI.

But as I stood watching, a troop of several hundred children came out of a side street and marched proudly round the shop, singing. They walked six abreast, led by a boy of ten or thereabouts. Hanging from each shoulder was a box containing brushes, bottles, and polishing-cloths. They were the "shoe-shiners" of Seoul.

Their strong, pure voices rang out above the din of lorries, Bren-gun carriers, and other noisy vehicles. They marched fast, the smallest in front, chanting a chorus which was taken up with great vigour by the taller end of the column.

Every day at 3 p.m. the corporation of shoe-shine boys used to march through the streets and congregate on some rough ground at the end of the city. They sang their national anthem and anti-communist choruses. The young Korean police-lieutenant who had organised them—beggars and thieves and strays—into this proud and homogeneous band, used to meet and instruct them daily, telling them how to give a good example of honesty, cleanli-

13. INDIA: Sculpture on a temple at Bubaneshwar

12. SIAM: This fearsome statue stands guard over a temple in Bangkok

14. SIAM: Children playing among
the statues of a temple

15. INDIA: A beggar asks for alms

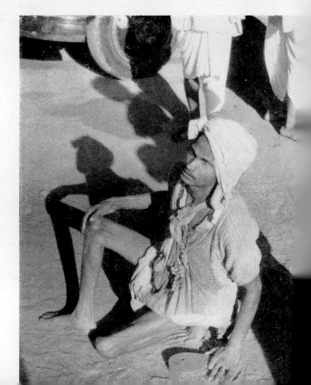

ness, and so forth, informing them shortly of the military, political, and economic situation, and reciting a chapter out of the lives of people born poor who had become famous. A recent programme covered Lincoln, Edison, and Joan of Arc. After their lecture the children would disperse still singing, to practise their lowly trade of shoe-polishing, the only career open to a generation of children that was utterly indigent and abandoned to its own devices.

We passed on to another building whose frontage had been much damaged by shell-fragments, and climbed a wide but banister-less staircase. Girls in uniform were going up and down, for this was the headquarters of Seoul's policewomen. In a big office hung with Sten guns, a number of women were seated round a table. Most of them were ugly, with hard, impassive, energetic faces. Going down a corridor, we passed a herd of sad-looking creatures, very much made-up—the outcome of a recent raid; there are fifteen thousand prostitutes in Seoul. At last we came to a small room where an officer of about fifty greeted us. She had a frank, smiling face. Rising, she saluted us and signed to us to sit down. We were in the presence of the Colonel of the Seoul Women Police. Sitting squarely in her whitewood chair she looked straight at us.

"You've come from Japan?"

I nodded and she went on: "Well. I suppose you like the Japanese. I may tell you that personally I would sooner be fighting the Japanese than the Communists. I spent ten years in prison under the Japanese occupation. They tortured me (she held out her hands, from which the nails had been torn). I had a child in prison and it died from want of care. All our troubles come from those people. They disturbed our thousand-year-old peace. They wanted to change our ways. . . ."

This is an opinion widely held in Korea.

But I wanted the Colonel to talk of more immediate matters and asked: "What do you do exactly?"

She got up and walked about the room. "You may know that prostitution is illegal in Seoul. Yet the numbers increase every day. As things are, a girl has to be heroic to stay decent. If she is alone, or worse still, if her family is dependent upon her, she can't earn enough to live. Prostitution is her only chance. We make raids every day. My idea is not to punish them but to try to change them. Unfortunately our means are so restricted that so far we

H

have been mainly repressive. Many of them become members of our organisation. You'll see."

She called out loudly: "Barbara! Barbara!" and sat down again.

"The name Barbara may surprise you. It was the name an American captain gave her. She was his mistress and his servant. Her husband had vanished the second time the town was invaded. She had just had a child. She lay in the ruins of her house until a demolition squad found her. The child was dead. They looked after her, and she met and fell in love with this American officer. He was a married man. One day he suddenly left Korea; she was utterly stranded. She then took up with a sergeant who was killed in the MacArthur offensive. After that . . . we picked her up in the street. She was ill and needed nursing. She has become my orderly."

A girl with large black eyes, her breasts tightly enclosed in a narrow khaki shirt, her hair coiled neatly round her head, appeared and stood to attention.

"Hullo, Barbara," I said.

"Hullo, sir," she replied rigid in her uniform.

Those who have suffered most in the war are the students. In the half-ruined medical school about fifty young men and women were working with three antiquated microscopes "Made in Japan". Their text-books were half in German, half in Japanese. I watched a class of a dozen boys who were taking an exam. They were drawing anatomical figures on a blackboard; a young American officer was in charge.

One of them, his face covered with ink, scratched his stiff black hair. "What are you going to do later?" I asked him. "Oh!" he said, "how can any Korean say what he may or may not do? At the moment all the medical students are sent to the armies as soon as they are trained. I shall be off in a few months."

Unfortunately the training in question is too brief and rudimentary to be of any use. The doctor of the Korean unit attached to the French had studied for only three months.

They have practically nothing, no books, no professors, no laboratories. There is no lack of corpses but you still have to learn anatomy.

·   ·   ·   ·   ·

In the centre of a big park, its trees ruined and burnt by napalm, stood a building almost untouched by gun-fire. This was the big agricultural school that had survived two successive invasions, and it was here that I had hoped to meet young men of my own age and to talk with them of the things that interest all young men.

I wanted the rambling conversations such as I had had in America, in Mexico, in Japan, everywhere, the sort that would give me an idea of what young Koreans were thinking. I was to come up against a wall of silence.

Some of them knew English but that did not serve. One big fellow in glasses, flushed and obviously most uncomfortable, told me, through the interpreter, that he was twenty-two, born in Suwon where his father sold ices and cakes during the summer and worked at the town hall during the winter. He had been at the school two years and would stay there three years more. When he left he expected to get an agricultural appointment under the Government as his sight was too bad for the Army.

The others were equally formal. Nothing of what they read, what they felt about the war, or their Government, or Americans, or the United Nations, or the Chinese, the Russians, the Japanese, democracy! In despair I begged them to ask me questions, whereupon they began to chatter noisily among themselves and then turned to me with blank faces, closed mouths. The silence seemed heavier than before! I could do nothing but get up and go. The director apologised. No doubt it was to the police of this so-called democratic state and the swift and implacable justice of Mr Syngman Rhee, whose portrait dominated the encounter, that I owed this array of sealed lips!

On the Seoul road a luminous sign enjoined the soldiers to "Take care of your uniforms. The rates pay for them."

I spent a fortnight in this land of South Korea where there was so much to see and to learn.

The night before I left, the sirens screamed over the town. It was eight years since I had heard their lugubrious, unforgettable cries. Seoul was fully lit as usual, the sky was clear, the moon shining splendidly. I got up and opened the window; the rumble of distant lorries came to me and the rat-tat of a typewriter next door. The broken walls were clearly visible. How was it that the enemy did not bomb this and other such obvious targets? A faint explosion sounded. What an odd war! Was there a tacit agreement between the parties? No doubt a Chinese bombardment would mean a United Nations bombardment beyond the Yalu?

The sirens howled again. I went back to my sleeping-bag. Next day two lines in *Stars and Stripes*, the American Army's daily, announced that a single unidentified plane had dropped two bombs on the outskirts of the city.

And here I was again on the icy tarmac of K 16. A cheerful group of Americans on leave chattered and laughed. We got into the plane. My neighbour was reading a magazine article thickly headed: "Paris! City of Sin!" He seemed deeply interested. We got talking, and he asked me a lot of questions about France and told me that in his opinion "Pinay is the man you want." Everyone was numbed with cold, and the classic mugs of coffee handed round this time by a tall, thin, wan-looking steward, were more than welcome. Dense fog was all about us. A light flashed; we began to lose height.

A few moments later I gratefully removed my belt; we were in Tokio.

25

Aliette's Triumph

IT WAS on the day following my return that the collection of dresses designed by Aliette was given its public showing. The newspapers announced it with a flourish of trumpets.

The vast drawing-room of the *Tokio-Kaikan* was completely full. An argument was going on in the wings. "Pay us!" shouted a mannequin, an exceptionally pretty, half-Chinese girl. "No! Presently!" "Now, at once!" "Certainly not." "You are a thief!"

Aliette was not the only one to have difficulties! The Dress Show started nevertheless. Coloured floodlights were trained on to the entrance; a piano broke out, a loudspeaker blared forth, the first model appeared. Frocks for the summer, for cocktails, for the afternoon, for small dinner-parties, for the evening, for grand occasions. Sitting by Aliette in the front row, I squeezed her hand in admiration and congratulation. Every dress had a name: "Sous les toits de Paris", "Ginza-Champs-Élysées". . . .

At the end of the first half everyone applauded. During the entr'acte a troup of little dancers performed a ballet. Over their stiff skirts they wore stays; it was an advertisement for a corset-making firm. The Japanese certainly have a strong publicity sense!

Second half: tailored suits, top-coats, highly elegant dresses made out of those wonderful Japanese silks. Aliette was nervous and fidgeting on her chair. "They're disgusting. Look! Another dress not ironed! It *is* so discouraging."

"Don't worry," I told her. "Nobody will notice." And the show ended with two superb wedding-dresses.

Great enthusiasm. What an odd country! Did any Japanese girl ever dream of being married in white? Yet these were the two dresses the organisers were most keen on.

Under fire from a crowd of flash photographers, Aliette was led

117

on to the stage and a little girl presented her with a superb bouquet of white flowers.

The applause went on and on. The crowd gathered about the foot of the stage and stared up at Aliette. Touched, she returned thanks in French. She had taken so much trouble, worked so hard. . . .

Last day in Tokio. We had taken our tickets for Hong Kong. Final twists and wriggles of our Japanese friends who did not wish to pay us our money. After a long and exhausting discussion, we got it a few hours before we left.

The editor of *Soen*, the mannequins and the interpreter came to see us off, bringing gifts, as custom enjoins. At Kobe we went on board the *Straat Makassar*, a brand new ship, and a few hours later the hills of Kobe were receding in the lovely spring sunlight. Leaning on the rail, we watched, a little sadly, the shores of this astonishing land vanish. The life we had lived there for the last three months had been difficult and tiring but also passionately interesting. No longer should we hear the clatter of the wooden sole or the deafening back-firing of Tokio taxis. We shall always remember the hard-working masses staring at the television shops, the men who leave their offices to watch the strip-tease shows for hours on end, their faces utterly blank, the women who kneel, polishing shoes, at street corners. But at the moment there was only one thing that really mattered to us: *sleep*.

26

An Excursion into China

THERE were only twelve passengers on this little Dutch steamer: two elderly American couples, an Australian husband and wife with whom we shared a table, a tall and elegant Chinaman, a huge Japanese with a greasy face, and two gluttonous Filippinos. We didn't see much of them; we slept day and night.

One morning a mountainous coast-line loomed up through the mist, and a sailing junk came to meet us; Hong Kong is the only large port where the pilots use sail. A man stepped on board. A long rope was hitched to the junk in which a bony-looking Chinese was sitting by the tiller silently watching the smoke of his cigarette curl in the still air. He wore a very large hat which hid his face. We proceeded slowly into the bay, passing other steamers and multitudes of other junks, some of which, with their high forecastles, resembled the caravels of old. The mist slowly cleared, and on our left arose the heights of Victoria Island. Before them was an imposing row of houses; the Hong Kong and Shanghai Bank being the largest.

Aliette, thrilled as usual, ran from one side of the deck to the other, dashed up on to the bridge and down again, and seizing me by the arm cried, "Isn't it really marvellous?"

Plainly, my "Yes" did not carry conviction, for she exclaimed, "Oh, you! You have no feeling for beauty." How often have I heard the very phrase apropos of a house, an ornament, a landscape, a man.

On either side of a gorge, up which a funicular railway crawled, ranged terraces of large buildings, smaller white buildings, houses set among trees. The *Straat Makassar* cast anchor, and the police arrived in their motor launch. Two tall Englishmen whom Aliette called "peculiarly ugly" examined our passports with great care and handed them back disdainfully. As soon as they were gone a crowd of junks clustered round: yells, jostling, much flourishing of the arms. Women in short trousers shrieked as they plied the long poles that directed their craft. On their backs unfortunate babies that the least jerk would toss into the water squeaked and whimpered. Dozens of coolies swarmed on to the *Straat Makassar*, leaping nimbly along the gangway, and the dance of the junks continued. Finally their sails were lowered, and half-naked children busied themselves with chop-sticks and rice-bowls. Little girls with long, black pigtails threw all their weight on to the bamboo poles that started the junks moving; soon the brown sails were being unfurled, the pulley-blocks creaking. . . .

Aliette had assured me that our luggage was all packed, yet I found a lot of things lying about the cabin and had to push them anyhow into a valise.

A tug brought us to Victoria Island. A sharp wind whipped our faces with spray. I spent the fifteen minutes of our passage counting and recounting our endless baggage. We landed on a small jetty pompously entitled the Queen's Pier. André Castel, the cultural attaché at Hong Kong, was waiting for us. We had some good times with him in Japan. He offered to put us up. A big square, lined with arcades and full of little English cars, opened out. After the bitter Japanese winter, it was pleasant to breathe the already milder air of the first March days.

In the middle of the square stood a big white rectangle of stone, the Memorial to the dead of the two wars. A Chinese policeman, most British in manner, ceremoniously directed the traffic, which was a dense conglomeration of cars and rickshaws. The rickshawmen were small and barefooted with hugely muscled calves; their cry of warning was shrill and metallic. Everything looked very clean and neat. A wide avenue takes us up towards Victoria Peak. Birds were singing in the luxuriant foliage.

That evening we strolled down again by the Queen's Road. The Chinese women wear tight, thin dresses opening at the side, sometimes so high that you see their thighs at every step. A blaze of neon lights illuminated a row of booths and little shops. The

windows were crowded with every sort of thing—ornaments in
gold or silver, jade, watches, fountain-pens, bags, bits of material.
They were offered at ridiculously low prices, and even so one had
to bargain or else lose face. Aliette was in ecstasies before every
shop-front. She would dash in without warning me so that I
walked on imagining her behind me. When she found something
truly "marvellous", she would run after me, drag me back willy-
nilly to the coveted object, ask what it cost, and exclaim loudly, to
the great astonishment of the vendor, that it was "really given
away". One day she was innocent enough to say to a little jeweller
whose entire stock she had been through, "All the same, you do
sell things too cheap." The man smiled grimly.

We dined at a small restaurant that did not seem too clean. The
fat proprietor poured us out copious draughts of tea and a waiter
brought pork wrapped in jam, a strange fish cut very small, rice,
and a fish soup. It was, we were told, the current Canton menu.
There was also Chinese bread, a shiny, crustless ball that looked
alarmingly indigestible. We walked back past hundreds of booths
that let out nauseating smells of dried fish and maybe of the
famous centenarian eggs that are such a delicacy in China!

We called on the French Consul. He gave us a hasty few
minutes. "You see," he explained, "half my time is taken up with
people passing through. Of course it's not so bad when they are
personalities like Duhamel, or Romains, or Paul Reynaud. . . ."

One afternoon we went with Castel and other friends to visit
the "New Territories". Captain André, the young woman whom
all the papers praised so tremendously for the wonderful work
she did as a doctor and a helicopter pilot in Indo-China, was in
our party. She was most charming and unaffected.

The ferry runs every ten minutes between Victoria and Kow-
loon, the chief "New Territory" town on the Chinese mainland.
We took it and proceeded by way of wide avenues cut by filthy,
crowded little side-streets. Over the houses are large advertisements, and the shops bear luminous signs even by daytime. You
would almost think it was Manhattan. Nothing but jewels and
bric-à-brac, curio shops where you can buy junk for ha'pennies and
vases at £300, and ivories, cheap or priceless; money-changers
who will buy your dollars and give you any currency you want;
tailors who will make you a suit in the best English cloth in

twenty-four hours for £12; jewellers who will finish any job with incredible speed. . . .

An old Citroën carried us farther inland. It was Sunday, and a stream of cars flowed along the narrow hill-road. Every driver in Hong Kong was abroad, and where would he go but on the classic "New Territories" excursion? We discovered with delight, between the valleys and the hills, what must surely have been the true Chinese landscape. Below us lay little dykes and tiny square rice-fields, where the great black buffaloes were ploughing, followed by women, bent beneath their big straw hats with blue hat-bands twisted round them. I found it very moving to see all Pearl Buck come to life. Without ever raising her head, sunk in the mud up to her knees, calling from time to time to her buffaloes, a black-garbed woman would trudge to and fro, patiently following the furrows that open and close again in the water-logged earth. Farther away, in a little port, beside the junks whose sails now were furled, other women squatted on their heels, selling the big crabs that they draw alive out of their creels. Dirty-faced children in black overalls ran to us, holding out their hands and murmuring some—to us incomprehensible—plaint. Aliette's heart was softened towards a lovely girl; she gave her a coin and received a sweet smile of thanks. Whereupon a mob of children scampered round us.

"No, I won't," Aliette said. "You're not a bit pretty."

"Surely," I put in, "that would be a reason to help them. A pretty, charming girl can always get away with it."

"Possibly," she retorted. "But I would do any mad thing for a beautiful person even if it was unjust."

The children's hands became pressing, insistent, rough. But this was nothing to what we were to find in India.

A convoy of Bren guns went by. A long column of young English soldiers debouched from a side-road, their packs and bazookas on their backs. They were off to manœuvres on the frontier; already we could see the batteries and the tanks and the lorries camouflaged under their big nets. The men marched quickly in spite of the heat. Aliette pronounced them "particularly ugly"; they were small, thin, and freckled.

Nearer the frontier we were stopped by a police officer and his men, armed with sub-machine guns. We could drive no farther, so we got out and went for a country walk. Aliette waited for us on the road, cursing her high heels. At the top of a little peak over a small fort (we could just see the loopholes) floated the English flag. Women in wide black trousers, tight blouses and big, blue-edged hats, were working on the paths, in the rice-fields, by the wells, or chatting among themselves as they trotted hither and thither.

In a hamlet, close to the frontier, was a farm that smelt like a French farm. Long-haired dogs slept in the sun beside archaic ploughs; children were snivelling and rubbing their eyes; women were returning from the well, each with her two buckets slung across her shoulders on a pole; over every door were draped pink papers inscribed with ideograms: charms to avert the evil spirits; hens scratched and pecked in the black earth.

There were some good-looking houses owned by rich Englishmen. Jaguars and shining black Rolls-Royces waited by the front doors. These pleasantly wooded hills make excellent settings for the well-to-do of Victoria. Here they can spend their week-ends if they can no longer go for excursions as they used to do, to Canton or elsewhere. The trouble, however, is the water-supply, which has to be brought from a great distance. In the event of war, a bomb on the Hong Kong reservoirs would be a winner.

Evening had come. Thousands of lights glimmered. We left this Western enclave inside peasant China and returned to Victoria. The lovely bay was dotted with every sort of craft. A big American aircraft-carrier had just cast anchor, and dozens of launches were carrying men in white caps ashore. Which meant an immediate drop in the value of the dollar.

27

Looking for Gambling-hells in Macao

OF THE three little boats that ply between Hong Kong and Macao we chose the oldest and least comfortable—in other words, the cheapest. The smoke from its funnel blackened the clear air; the hull quivered violently; we weaved in and out between a group of huge three-sailed junks that danced about and plunged their noses into the water. We were the only Europeans on board; I took a look round. In a cubby-hole behind our cabin I found half a dozen rifles and a chest containing grenades and four tommy-guns. A small Chinese in a white coat, passing down the alley-way, gave me a push with his shoulder, banged the cubby-hole door to and turned the key of a big padlock.

"Not allowed go there," he said in his stumbling English.

I asked him what the arms were for. He snapped back: "Communists! Pirates!" and I remembered that the papers had spoken of a fishing-boat held up and attacked recently by Communists. Aliette glanced uneasily at me. For a long while we steamed past the wrinkled wave-like line that marks the presence of innumerable floats supporting anti-submarine nets—the division between the two powers' territorial waters. The first mountain chains of Communist China were quite close to us, shutting out the horizon. A grey vessel, a crane on its prow, was repairing the nets. Junks slipped by, heeling over in the breeze. The usual women, their babies on their backs, squatted by the bar that supported the big, groaning tiller.

Silently, brown sails and black sails glided by; a flat tongue of land jutted out into the sea. At the extreme point one could make out a large, low building in the Spanish style, and beyond that, above grey ramparts, bright-looking houses, white or deep yellow, with arches and black wrought-iron gates. The boat passed round the peninsula and sailed into a narrow stretch of water that ran up towards the hills. Not a chimney anywhere to be seen against the pale gold sky, not another ship, nothing resembling the unceasing activity of Hong Kong. We felt as though we were visiting a fishing village.

Our steamer berthed alongside a wooden wharf perpendicular to Macao's long, northern quay. Here were large advertisements in Portuguese and Chinese, two moustached immigration officers, tightly buttoned into their linen uniforms, to examine our passports, and a stout gentleman, born of Portugal and China, who hailed us in a lingua franca composed of Portuguese, English, Chinese, French, Spanish, and German. Aliette, having a gift for languages, made out that he was offering to be our taxi-driver and guide, to show us Macao "by day and by night" and to introduce us to the grandest restaurant in town. Not being able to afford these luxuries, we hired a cycle-rickshaw to take us to the Communist frontier, which is the great thing to see in Macao.

I felt as though I was in the south of Japan. Trundling quietly in our osier basket, our Chinese swaying nonchalantly from side to side, we reached a little square surrounded by the high walls of ancient houses and the towers of an old Romanesque church. The bells were ringing the Angelus. We wandered down a boulevard shaded by immense tamarisks beside quiet waters where the junks' sails spread translucent in the setting sun. On our right, half-hidden in the little gardens fresh with flowers, were houses, small here and arcaded and covered with ivy and climbing roses. The tiles of the roofs gleamed scarlet. Over one door was an inscription, scored and dulled by time: *Casa di Misericordia*. A green shutter opened and we got a glimpse of the white coif of a Sister of Saint-Vincent-de-Paul. There is no sound but the faint creak of the cycle's pedals. Silence and still waters, no trace of life, a numbness, a heavy peace—that is the impression we gathered in this scrap of Portugal transplanted in China.

Our cyclist speeded up; we were near the frontier. The cracked, tarred road ended, *chevaux de frise* barred further progress. A couple of hundred yards ahead, the Red Flag was flying half-masted because of the recent demise of Stalin. I jumped out and prepared my camera. A wild shout made us jump. An enormous negro brandishing a rifle and still yelling at the top of his voice was rushing towards us. He stopped and, pointing to my camera, made it plain that photographs were forbidden there. He glanced at Aliette, smiled, and walked slowly away. We had no notion that Macao was defended by Mozambique negroes!

All the same I could not resist it; hurriedly I took my snapshot. It wasn't every day one got such a chance. Going back we met a patrol of these black giants. They all looked equally good-natured.

Indeed it is Andalusia: wide, empty avenues, lined with great trees, two-storeyed houses with little balconies filled with flower-pots, high wrought-iron gates. Four kilometres one way, three the other, and we had been all round Macao.

My wife, who has read Dekobra, wanted to visit a gambling-hell. Night had fallen, and our cycle-rickshaw had returned us to the centre of the town. Aliette disapproved of this mode of transport; she got most indignant and insisted on my getting out and walking up the smallest hill to save the cyclist's legs.

"I won't ever get into a thing drawn by a man again!" she firmly declared.

"Don't be silly," I told her. "If you don't, you keep the poor fellows from earning their living."

"I don't care. It makes me too unhappy."

"And you never think of the men who toil in ships' engine-rooms or do any other of the painful work, and even risk their lives to produce the things you buy and that you must have for your comfort?"

"I don't worry about those people," she rejoined with relentless logic, "because I don't see them."

We came to a tall six-storeyed building. The commissionaire was a splendid Sikh who wore his beard rolled up in a net. We went into the gambling-hell. On each floor was a huge room full of tables covered in green baize and figures. We were terribly disappointed. There was no crowd of gamblers, there was, indeed, nobody! Fat, uncommonly ugly women were perched on high stools; they had numbers on their chests. We took our place beside the one and only customer. He was a little Chinese, thin as a rake, nervous as a cat, smoking Craven A after Craven A, his legs and knees jerking miserably. He fiddled with a meagre roll of notes which, after much hesitation, he put on this number or that. Every ten minutes the stout woman on the stool behind his table would call out something and shake her dice-box. When he lost the Chinese snapped his fingers, and his legs and knees would shake more than ever. So much for the gambling-hell.

We dined hastily. Outside, elegant Portuguese ladies in flowered frocks and mantillas were taking the air. Presently a torchlighted funeral passed, all the mourners in white, as is the Chinese custom, the coffin richly decorated and followed by old women in big hats so overwhelmed with grief that girls had to support them. For a few moments the torches brightened the street, and then again the stillness, the dusk.

Returning to our ship, we found the quayside brilliantly lit and alive with bustling coolies. A man carrying a bundle of books followed us and whispered to me in the alley-way: "Filthy pictures?"

I went into our cabin and said to Aliette: "If you want to see some pretty photographs ask the gentleman."

"Idiot!" she answered. "He's selling books!"

The man handed her one and she turned over a few leaves.

"Well? What about it?" she said and then discovered inset in the pages, a series of photographs.

"Oh!" she cried in consternation, flicking them over.

And suddenly burst out laughing. The man goggled at us and again offered to sell the books. Aliette gave him one astonished look. The engines were throbbing, the ship began to quiver, and our gentleman took to his heels.

Not a light to be seen on the opposite shore. As we left the wharf a big motor ship started out after us, a strange, perplexing shape. Here and there our own lights picked out the floating junks, asleep like great ducks upon the still sea. The lapping of the water against the stern and the dull thud-thud of the engines were the only sounds that broke the mystery of the night. The lights of Macao faded, becoming no more than a blurred reflection on the black water. We gazed back at the shores of the great continent which no one can now visit and for which we felt a kind of wistful, unreal nostalgia.

The hours slipped by; night and its coolness cradled us into lethargy and sleep. Then suddenly it was dawn, and we were back in Hong Kong.

28

En Route for the
Venice of the East

BEFORE leaving Hong Kong we piled most of our
things into four big bags and sent them off to Paris. Aliette, terri-
fied of moth, was so heavy-handed with the naphthalene that it
will take months before the smell wears off.

The modest sum of £10 a head took us on board an old cargo-
boat bound for Bangkok.

For a day and a night we steamed past the deserted coast of
Indo-China. Not a village, not a beat; at night utter darkness. I
looked in vain, through my field-glasses, for the least sign of life,
and thought sadly of the many young Frenchmen who were fighting
and dying beyond that thickly treed shore. The heat was oppressive, and the lady passengers—six Americans, usually so voluble—
lay exhausted in their deck-chairs. Aliette sunbathed from morning till night. Despite my warnings, the snob-fashion for a bronzed
skin brought her back in the evening to our stifling cabin in pain,
all red and swollen, and I spent the night coating her with all the
oil I could find in the dining-saloon. Moaning, she swore that she
would never do it again.

The last day of our run the sea became dirty in patches; plank-
ton, apparently. Farther off, schools of porpoises were playing and
great white gulls wheeled overhead. For a long time the Siamese
coast was indistinguishable from the horizon, so flat was it. Our
ship slowed down beside a small steamboat, to await the full tide
before crossing the bar. We watched until, at the stroke of a gong,
we were permitted to cross it and then started to ascend the
muddy waters of the river. The banks were flat and covered with
tall coconut-trees.

Our next halt was at Paknam. The immigration staff came on board. The chief officer spoke French and welcomed us with a kindly smile. Aliette admired his fine black eyes. The medical inspection followed and I found I had lost my certificate of inoculation for cholera and smallpox. This would mean no landing, so all I could do was to present Aliette's for the second time. It worked and we started off again. The river banks were thick with dense swamp vegetation; we could hear the song of birds and the grating noise of crickets. The heat, this early April day, was very heavy.

A bell rang for dinner. We could not miss that; it was our last certain meal. We were so hard up by now that, according to our calculations, we could only spend three days in Bangkok at the rate of one meal a day.

We reached the quay. A lot of little men, naked to the waist, got busy with the cargo. The neon lamps gave their skins a curious colour.

The Captain invited us to spend the night on board and we accepted with considerable relief. We hated arriving at night-time in an unknown town. Although it was so late, the Customs officers appeared and young men went through the cabins with their torches, pitilessly thorough, turning everything upside down. One of them cried out in triumph and exhumed from a valise of Aliette's a studded Mexican belt. The studs do give a certain suggestion of bullets, and all Aliette's powers of gesticulation were required to convince him of their innocence. He was, however, finally persuaded, and the search ended in an exchange of smiles.

Next morning—Bangkok: great avenues and luxuriant vegetation and little canals on which many sampans were floating. Whole families live on these boats and quantities of mangy dogs. It is a lively, laughing city. At every street corner a dozen pairs of muscular legs hang over the pedals of the cycle-rickshaws drawn up in the shade. A Buddhist priest, draped in his yellow robe, was taking the air under a parasol. The azalea bushes were full of singing birds. A few carriages went bumping by over the ruts. A boat was stuck in the mud, and beside it a naked child was weeping. In the "rue de la Paix" three oddly dressed policemen controlled a tangle of cycle-rickshaws, bicycles, motor bikes, cars, carriages, and pedestrians. At the end of an alley, by the river, we

I

found the French Embassy. We went into an office and were amazed: it was air-conditioned! Having been told of Monsieur G. D . . . .'s kindliness and good nature, we asked for him and were immediately received. He was a tall, slim, distinguished-looking man, slightly bald. We gave him a brief account of our tour and asked if it would be possible to rent a room in some private house. His secretary at once turned round and invited us to stay with her. Nicole de B . . . . was indeed to be the good angel of our stay. Her charm and happy temper remain as one of our best memories. Thanks to her we met all the members of the French colony, nice people, who, for once, got on well together. Bangkok can be very gay. Every night we went to dinner-parties; Aliette wore her real evening-dresses and we danced till long past midnight.

But, once again, our first concern on arrival in a new place was to find the best means of getting out of it. Until that was settled we couldn't enjoy ourselves. We had heard that the head of Thai Airways, the company that runs a weekly service to Calcutta, was a general and had done all his military training in France. So we started with the general. Nicole lent us her Vespa and we crossed the town, risking a dozen tumbles in the roads' deep ruts. Twice we were unlucky: the general had just gone off or had not yet returned. Bangkok telephones being of a somewhat erratic nature we could not make an appointment. We did not miss our chance, however, of seeing this curious city and its many temples.

We went from one to the other. Each had its own charm, here the "Emerald Buddha" seated on a golden throne in the Wat Phra Keo or Royal Temple, there the great tower of the Temple of the Dawn that stands on the water's edge and looks like an enormous monstrance reflected in the dull stream of the Menam, the "Mother of Waters", creator of Siam's prosperity and of which it is said: "He who drinks of its waters will always return." Or again there was the incomparable beauty of the modern Wat Benjamahopitr, whose golden roofs rose tier upon tier above white marble walls.

The rich and delicate decorations of these temples contrast very markedly with the austere surroundings of the priests. Simplicity is the first law of the Buddhist priesthood. Every Siamese adolescent enters it for a limited period, the vows being at no time binding. It is his opportunity for learning of the higher moral things of life. Every day we saw groups of such young men walking in their yellow togas, their heads and eyebrows shaven, through the streets or by the canals. The robe is the same for rich and poor, high and low, which makes for a complete absence of social distinction and for humility, as does the begging-bowl with which every priest goes from house to house, asking for the food that is never refused. To feed such men generously is, for the Siamese, to take out an insurance on eternity.

One afternoon in a temple garden, I watched some hard-faced priestlings officiate at a funeral. I ventured into the building itself but Aliette remained discreetly outside, talking in I don't know what language to the chauffeurs of the fine black limousines that had brought the family of the wealthy dead. The coffin, adorned with gold and precious stones, was in the middle of the hall. The thin and sickly-scented smoke of many censers rose about it. The congregation was dressed after the European style, men in white summer suits, their lapels gorgeous with decorations, the women in veils or mantillas and black taffeta frocks. No grief, no quiet, no meditation; they were chattering freely among themselves, and servants were handing round glasses of sparkling Coca-Cola. At the back, behind the coffin, some young priests, armed with gilded fans, crouched on a platform spread with carpets and recited psalms in the monotonous tones that remind one of the reading of the Koran in Mohammedan mosques. The fans swayed rhythmically before their plump faces. On and on they went, louder and louder chattered the guests. After what seemed a very long time, four men in white lifted the coffin on to their shoulders, and the procession, preceded by the priests in yellow, moved down the steps of the temple, past the cocoa-trees and the ornamental lake of green water and disappeared into that dark place where, by night, unseen of any stranger's eye, the body would be burned.

I found Aliette outside the entrance gate, sitting on the grass with a circle of admirers. She was writing down numbers on a sheet of paper.

"I am trying," she told me, "to work out for them what a Foca would cost in ticals."

At last we found General Chai. He offered me, in exchange for a write-up of his company, a very considerable reduction on our fares to Calcutta. Aliette took immediate advantage of this and sped off to the Bangkok shops to buy curios.

29

Round and About the Menam

SIAM's capital fully deserves to be called "The Venice of the East". At dawn on a day that promised to be scorching, the G. D.....s carried us off for a tour of the *klongs*, the canals on which half the population lives. This early hour is also the time when the malaria-carrying mosquitoes are abroad. We started out in a flat-bottomed boat that had the most deafening motor, and crossed the Menam with its mass of heterogeneous craft. The scene reminded me of Xochimelco. The houses on either side were of wood and built on piles, and a dense multitude of laden sampans and canoes were gliding up and down between them. By the shores, roots of mangroves twisted in the water. Priests went by in their frail skiffs. We zigzagged in and out whilst they pursued, unmoved, their lonely way.

In other little boats, so laden with fruit and vegetables that their gunwales were almost level with the stream, sat wrinkled old women, crop-haired, chewing betel. A booth, also built on piles, displayed a collection of large hats.

"Marvellous!" cried Aliette. "What lovely lampshades they would make!"

Children were bathing or paddling in the dark water, swimming out and clinging to the sides of our boat, tilting it most dangerously. We passed a temple entirely encrusted with blue mosaic and guarded by two hideous lions. Some of the canals are so narrow that the foliage closes above them, making a mysterious green roof over our heads; trunks of teak-trees, scarcely visible, glided swiftly along, propelled by the long poles of their riders.

132

Still farther on, barefooted Chinese were unloading baskets of rice from a barge. The baskets were slung on long poles which they balanced across their shoulders like a see-saw. Glimpses of a happy, care-free people.... Time passed; the crowd thinned; everyone was settling down to a long, sweet, drowsy day. ...

Aliette's afternoon siestas were spent lying under the electric fan reading all the books on Siam that she could discover. She soon knew so much that her friends were astonished, especially those friends in France who read her long and charming letters. What she sets down is never inexact and is always presented in its most attractive form. I ran about, chasing the visas we needed for our next stage and collecting materials for future articles.

For Thailand, the "land of the free", interests me prodigiously. It is perhaps the only Far Eastern country where no hatred or resentment is felt towards the white races. Forming a sort of blind alley in the midst of rival systems that have left their mark on its neighbours, it has never known "colonialism". Surrounded by fighting, twenty-three million people live peacefully on a fruitful soil, untouched by any major trouble, content. The price of this peace is a happy-go-lucky disorder, a corruption of its own peculiar kind, and an economic life that is typically undeveloped.

At the end of Bangkok's "Champs-Élysées", which was built in a few months during the Japanese occupation to allow the march-past of the "victorious" Siamese troops, is a monument containing an urn, and in the urn is a copy of the Constitution that the King gave his people after the *coup d'état* of 1932. Having become a monarch of the English school, the King's role is solely one of unification, which is singularly easy with a population that makes no claims, suffers no hardships and eats its fill. On the rare occasions when he appears in public he is a hieratic figure, unsmiling, apparently bored. At the end of film performances his photograph is invariably thrown on the screen and the national anthem is played. Propaganda of this sort may be a sign of popular disaffection. Such things have been known before. Chiang Kai-shek always had his portrait shown in the Chinese cinemas.

The crown has no connexion whatsoever with politics, which go from *coup d'état* to *coup d'état* between the three permanent rivals: the Army, the Navy, and the Police. Actually, these disturbances cause little bloodshed. The point is: which of the three forces, firing their guns into the air on the banks of the Menam, will make most noise and so gain most prestige? Another symptom of the happy-go-lucky nature of this tragi-comedy is the sight of the machine-gunners earning pocket-money from the spectators by allowing them to fire the guns at five ticals a burst.

The Government is more or less democratic. It exercises certain controls, notably on rice, which is the chief product of the country and usually provides a surplus for export. The rulers fix its price, which is very low, so low indeed that in 1952 production fell and public accounts no longer balanced. To control and decontrol and partially control the banks and exchanges seems to be the financial policy. The people ask little, continue to be well-fed and contented, the rate of exchange is relatively high; the rulers can profiteer without doing much harm in matters that have, so far, always yielded such a good profit.

Modernisation is still in embryo; the public services of which we are often so proud in Europe, scarcely exist. Occasionally the Government makes a grand gesture and orders a super-electric plant, or decides that Bangkok must have television. These grandiose plans do not always come off.

But strategically the great plain of Siam, rice-granary of the Far East, set as it is between continental China and the oil of Indonesia, the rubber and the tin, occupies a highly important position. In these hypersensitive, not to say nervy, parts of the world it is difficult to say what sudden incident might not upset the chessboard of which Siam is a vital square. The local seers have prophesied that in the year 2500 of the Buddhist era sensational events will shake the world. Now, in 1953, we are in the year 2496. But remembering their easy life and fine Buddhist tradition, disregarding the esoteric prediction, it is possible that the Siamese may some day have a life both modern and worthy of their past without falling into the extreme passions that have torn their neighbours and wrought so much harm.

30

Aliette wants to smoke Opium

ONE evening Nicole invited us to the popular theatre. It was apt to move from place to place and was difficult to find. Usually it was in one of the markets.

We went through a sort of porch. In one corner a black-eyed child was selling cigarettes by the wavering light of an acetylene lamp. The mangy dogs were everywhere, snuffling through the market-day refuse. Buddhism forbids them to be killed, and rabies is a real menace in Bangkok. We found ourselves in a huge shed. The heat was beyond words; the smell of urine caught one's throat; crossing the hall we held our handkerchiefs to our noses. The audience consisted of women chewing betel and running their fingers through their short, stubbly hair, and of men laughing and spitting and eating God alone knows what. The stage was brilliantly lit; the rough-and-ready scenery suggested the inside of a palace; half a dozen wonderfully bedizened actors moved back and forth, talking in whining voices that made the spectators laugh.

The show lasted two hours, and when it was over we decided to finish the evening in an opium den. There are three in Bangkok at prices that vary, in principle, according to their elegance. They are, in fact, much the same.

The one we visited is near the centre of the Chinese quarter. This is the only part of Bangkok where the shop fronts are lit by neon lights. The cinemas have large illuminated signs that flash on and off; the streets are full of people strolling about or sitting at cafés or on the kerbs. We went down a dark little side-lane and

135

came to a low door over which burned a dim light. Leprous walls and a long passage, a little courtyard, a stove on which a big cauldron was simmering, watched by a matron of vast proportions, generously décolletée, a very big room divided up by screens, low beds covered with mats. On each bed a half-naked man crouched, staring vaguely into space, his skin waxy in the light of the two bulbs that hung from the ceiling. There was a sour and not at all engaging smell of perspiration. In one place a huge bony fellow squatted kneading his pellet of opium and cramming it into the bowl of his long pipe. His forehead glistened with sweat, his eyes were very bright. He lighted his pipe and put it to his lips, the muscles of his throat contracted and the skin of his chest stretched so tightly over his ribs that every line of them was visible; he took a deep breath, laid down the pipe, kept the smoke in his lungs for a long time and, finally, exhaled it very slowly. His whole body relaxed and he sank back with an air of extreme well-being. The stout matron brought him a teapot and a little bowl.

"It doesn't attract me any more," Aliette said. "I don't believe I could feel the least pleasure in this smell and this lugubrious light. It might be a dormitory at Buchenwald."

A large butterfly fluttered about the lamp. The man watched it vaguely. Aliette added: "Vice I can understand in gracious and delicate surroundings, but——" and we left this painful scene.

Our country-house life was ending. One last cocktail-party at the G. D . . . . s whom we thanked most gratefully for their charming and spontaneous kindness. We were off in search of further adventures. In a few hours we should be in India, the land of which we had both dreamed since childhood.

The night was still pitch dark; the spluttering of a motor sounded in the New Road: it was the Thai Airways coach. The conductor put in our luggage; sadly we said good-bye to Nicole. By the dim light of one small lamp, we could just discern the inside of the ancient bus. It stopped frequently to pick up passengers: two Europeans speaking Yiddish, tall Indians in floating robes, women in saris, children with black-smudged eyelids, Burmese with rolled beards, and long hair tucked under many-coloured turbans. Gradually we filled up.

The sky grew greyish, and then suddenly it was dawn. Bangkok aerodrôme is highly modern. By the tarmac is a large café bordered with flowers; huge petrol-tanks stand by gigantic "Constellations"; mechanics dart about them. Stout Dutchmen lay stretched out in blue leather arm-chairs, their placidity and their white, freckled skins in strange contrast to the dirty, evil-smelling, and sometimes fierce-eyed and alarming Burmese. A flat and skinny Englishman was talking to a little Siamese in a white coat; a solitary Chinese was walking up and down. He wore rimless glasses and carried a large portfolio most impressively stamped with initials. A splendid Indian woman in red draperies was giving the breast to her baby. Her arms were richly laden with bangles of gold and precious stones. The child reached up its plump fingers trying to grasp at the gold ring that adorned its mother's beautifully shaped nose.

A loud-speaker growled and we climbed into the DC 4 of Thai Airways. The engines throbbed and roared and we were off. Aliette was chewing gum in silence. Well! We are in the sky and faced with a copious breakfast. The water tasted of tea, the coffee tasted of water, and the tea tasted of nothing at all.

31

The First Nightmares
of Our Honeymoon

THROUGH the porthole we watched the impenetrable
Burmese jungle and shivered a little. Rangoon! The heat was very
great. Two policemen stood guard over our plane. We went into
the aerodrome's overcrowded hangars in an attempt to find a little
coolness under the wheezy electric fans. Large blackboards gave
statistics of the daily deaths from plague and cholera. A ragged,
evil-smelling crowd climbed into the little twin-engine machines
that fly inland. So many towns are encircled by the Communists
that there is frequently no means of travel in Burma except by air.
Two nuns in coifs, their pink cheeks shining with sweat, were
arguing with a beggar. He clawed and clung to their rosaries.

And again the jungle. A month ago a plane disappeared into
it and was never seen again. Then the sea. The air was fresher,
and I became deaf; we ran into air-pockets, and Aliette's face
went green. We were over the mouths of the Ganges. Aliette was
feeling worse and got out her little oiled-paper bag. I was quite
all right and told her so, to which she replied crossly: "Oh! you!
You never feel anything."

A flat, naked expanse, cut by dozens of narrow streams of dirty,
muddy water. It was just like an anatomical section seen through
a microscope, a sinuous network of canals spreading unevenly
over a stretch of grey mud. A few coconut-trees suddenly appeared, forming a tiny oasis about a group of mud huts. Our plane
started to lose height, and to Aliette's great satisfaction, I began
to feel squeamish. The ground looked dry. It was divided into
small squares. The coconut-trees grew bigger; I could distinguish

men. Then the smallest details of the landscape grew clear; the
cabin door opened, and an intolerable burst of heat exploded in
our faces. India!

A single spot of colour in the sun-baked aerodrome: the cockade
of an Air France plane just off to Paris. How far away Paris
seemed.

Our disembarking was supervised by fat-bellied officials in khaki
uniforms after the English style. A bamboo stick and a pair of pig-
skin gloves lay on every desk. The Indians often seem most
anxious to copy, even to the point of making themselves ridiculous, the ways of the people of whom they generally speak so ill.
Our luggage was brought out, and at once a dozen ragged men
tried to snatch at it. Aliette's valise was stained with brown paint;
furthermore, its handle had gone. Much discussion with the company's agent who promised to make the loss good.

"Monsieur Lapierre?"

We were being greeted by a smiling gentleman who introduced
himself as the French vice-consul, "Jean B . . . . I was told of your
arrival by wire and have come to meet you and to bring you your
mail."

We thanked him warmly and opened our letters with greedy
haste. Among them was a telegram from Renault announcing with
the utmost impertinence that we could not have the frigate
promised to us three months ago as it had been sold to the French
Ambassador in Indonesia. Nice behaviour! They might at least
have let us know sooner. Other firms were interested in our
Calcutta–Paris trip; we could have made arrangements with them.
For months we had given ourselves the greatest trouble in preparing our itinerary and scrupulously submitting it to the Renault's
agent in Tokio.

But first things first. We were in the heart of Calcutta; where
could we sleep that night? We did the rounds of the hotels and
the question was soon answered; they were all full and impos-
sibly expensive. We could do nothing but accept our new consular
friend's charming offer of a room in his flat.

Aliette opened her suitcase. Catastrophe! The cork of a bottle
of mercuro-chrome had popped and the stuff had all run out.
"You're wonderful, aren't you?" my wife remarked caustically,
"with your great experience of travelling. It didn't occur to you

before we took the plane that there might be differences of pressure. . . ."

We were both rubbing away furiously when our bell rang. The
assistant Commercial Attaché, Michel de C... a tall, thin,
intelligent-looking man, had just heard of our arrival and had
come to suggest that he should show us round Calcutta that night,
right away.

The day began badly. Why not finish it well? We accepted with
enthusiasm.

"If you want to understand India," our guide said, swerving to
avoid a man lying in the middle of the street, "you can't do better
than see Calcutta. All the problems of this huge country are
summed up in this one huge town. Everything—politics, eco-
nomics, social questions, religious questions, everything."

We drove quickly through a big park and came to an avenue
full of trams, cars, motor buses, rickshaws, and people on foot. We
then crossed over a big metal bridge which was also densely
crowded. Pressed against each other and the parapets were thousands of people carrying bundles or old valises tied up with string.
Heavy rickshaws passed by, drawn with difficulty by little, bony
creatures who seemed lost between the shafts and occupied by
fat men lying back luxuriously and showing their hairy thighs
between the folds of their robes. We reached the Howrah station.
Policemen in red tarbooshes blew their whistles and attempted to
control the utterly disordered traffic. Streams of men and women
were milling around, stepping over their fellows asleep on the
pavement.

In the great station-hall were whole families, dozens of them,
camping out beneath the neon lamps amidst excrement and refuse
of every kind. They have been here for months. Young women,
thin as skeletons, draped in scraps of grey linen, were giving the
breast to wretched, swollen-bellied babies. Their fragments of
washing were suspended by string from one lamp to another.
They had no means of living except to beg alms of the passing
travellers. Famished children were sucking at the skins of gourds,
picked up heaven knows where, or selling cigarettes spread out
on the tops of cases. Men were sleeping, their heads resting on a
stone, ghastly pale in the bluish glow. We stepped over their
bodies. Old men and infants gazed up sadly, murmuring their

"Backsheesh, mister," which they seem unable even to utter with conviction.

These were the refugees compelled to leave their homes because of Partition. They had found no place of refuge but this sordid hall. One young woman was sitting on her heels, heating some water. A small, bushy-haired child was wriggling about beside her. I watched her for a long time. One shoulder was bare; she moved slowly and carefully and kept her back very straight; she had a certain attraction. At last a little steam arose from the saucepan. The woman got up, gathered up a handful of rice from a fold of her robe and, crouching again, scattered it in the water. But the child threw out its arm and overturned the saucepan. The woman jumped up, gave us a furious look, slapped the child, who instantly started howling, and went off to fetch some more water. Baksheesh, Baksheesh... The refrain never ceased, painful, haunting. Leaving the station we were pursued by a whole troop of tatterdemalions and climbed quickly, horrified, into the car. The children tapped on the windows and the mudguards, and spread out in front of us, barring our way, crying, "Baksheesh, mister!" It was something to remember.

We drove on down a wide street that had a wall on one side and a railway track on the other. By the wall were rows of human beings squatting on the pavement.

"This is the quarter of the dying. This is where many of the people of Calcutta come to die. . . ."

"Charming!" said Aliette. She was plainly becoming less and less at her ease.

"A little farther on," continued our guide, "we shall see the place where the corpses are burnt. It is a curious sight."

We got out of the car at the Hoogly River. The night was dark, and we could see flames leaping up against the whiteness of a wall. I was not feeling very comfortable. Aliette, clenching her teeth, took my arm and Michel de C . . .'s also. We came to a small square; acrid-tasting smoke took us by the throat; we were near the funeral pyres. Two men were going towards them bearing, on a stretcher, a large white bundle. Black feet protruded from the shroud, and a head; we caught a glimpse of a terrible, ravaged face.

The kinsmen walked behind. They were talking amongst themselves without any apparent grief. A grossly fat dog, its mouth crammed with who knows what filth, ran between our legs. The smoke grew thicker; against the white wall the shadows of the dancing flames were reflected, distorted, fantastic. A blind child, seated under a tree, was crooning a plaintive, monotonous song. We followed the funeral procession and entered the enclosure where the fires were. On the left a heap of embers was already blackening; on the right a man, naked to the waist, was throwing branches on to a burning brazier. A head hung from it; a body contracted in the flames. A sharp crack: a skull had burst. We walked quickly through the hellish scene. Aliette, appalled, shut her eyes.

"Tell me when this horror is over."

Four bodies were lying on stretchers before the funeral pyres, ready for cremation. They had been dead barely two hours; in this climate the flesh corrupts quickly, and to avoid disastrous epidemics no time must be lost. Ashes swirled up and fell upon the families of the dead who remained utterly impassive, waiting for the fires to die for want of fuel. The smell was very bitter. An arm was flung madly up. Two men were having a heated argument. This, it seems, is a common incident; the one was accusing the other of not putting enough wood on his corpse. Two undertakers lighted a third pyre; their sweating skins shone in the blaze. They raised their stretcher and tilted its contents gently on to the ground; then removing the shroud they lifted the body, one by the arms, the other by the legs. It apears that they sometimes break the neck or the joints to avoid ugly contortions during the burning. The corpse was then laid on the fire and the flames began to crackle savagely. A woman, draped in a long, pale pink sari, her face half hidden by her veil, watched the scene with the utmost calm. When the piled-up wood and bones and flesh had become no more than a heap of ashes, she drew a little carved box from beneath her veil, bent over and without fear of scorching her long, thin fingers, gathered a handful of the dust and put it quickly in the box. The lid snapped to: slowly, she straightened herself, passed her blackened hand over her face and hurried away. Later on, no doubt, she would, as custom bids her, scatter the ashes in the sacred waters of the Ganges.

The infernal tour continued. We returned to the big bridge. On the shores of the river, skeleton-thin cows were cropping the miserable tufts of yellow grass that grew between the paving-stones. A *saddhu*, that is a sort of sage, deeply venerated, squatted, naked save for his loin-cloth, among a number of tins containing little growing plants. In another disused tin some repulsive-smelling incense was burning. He spat, and the betel juice made a stain like blood. Watched by a pious group of disciples, he waved his arms and, in a gesture of purification, smeared his body with streaks of some pale substance. His toothless mouth grimaced hideously and occasionally he jerked his head, and his long, oily hair floated about his shoulders.

We were now driving past a two-storeyed house where a ceremony was proceeding that it was difficult to see and, for an "unbeliever", dangerous to approach too closely. For safety's sake we had closed the windows of the car. A mass of people, their bodies striped in many colours, were gathered into a kind of big shed. They were dancing or jerking violently, in front of what looked like the grating of a lift-shaft. From this cage-like place, great flames flowed out illuminating most strangely the grotesque, crimson statues of the Goddess Kali. We saw no more; a man had caught sight of our car and was running forward with other fanatics who would have made short work of us if they could. We accelerated and disappeared into the district reserved to the "untouchables"—long rows of hovels stretching this way and that in a confusion of decaying alley-ways. Children were curled up on the ground, their heads in the gutter. Perhaps they were dead. Shrunken arms were held out to us, so many that charity could but fail before them. Dogs that were no more than skin and bone were nosing about in the rubbish; they growled as we passed. In this human jungle where everything is wretched, everything is hostile. Dreadful prostitutes caught at our sleeves, begging for cigarettes. What type of man can it be who takes these vile women into his pitch-dark hut?

All about the little temples were crowds worshipping the grotesque statue of Siva; peering through an open door, we saw it, brilliantly lit on its altar. The hour was already late; the roadways were filling up with outstretched figures. Millions of Indians sleep in the street.

So, very slowly, we passed through the mysterious city. Its ghastly scenes haunted us, and our first night in India was troubled by atrocious dreams.

32

First Encounters. These People frighten us . . .

CALCUTTA is a dreadful city. We decided to leave it and to travel southward to see the famous temples of Bubaneshwar, Puri and Konarak. Equipped with two bottles of tea, we returned to the dreadful station we had visited on our first evening. This time there was no one with us, and we were, I must admit, faintly apprehensive. We had been most seriously warned to take care on the trains, to double-lock the doors of our carriage, to open them on no pretext whatsoever. Thefts and murders occur frequently.

So there we were alone, carrying our little bags, in the big Howrah station surrounded by its wretched humanity. A gang of children rushed at us, and we could only be rid of them by going into the stationmaster's office. A man was working in the dim light; he received us politely and had us escorted to our carriage. The children dared not follow. Second class: we had both sides of quite a big apartment. I opened a door, and to my astonishment found a water closet and a shower! India is really very up to date. The ticket-collector, immaculate in white drill, came to welcome us and punched our tickets. Like most employees of the Indian Railways he was an Eurasian, a much envied and wholly detested class.

Waiting for the train to start, we strolled up and down the platform, watching the people with their bundles, their canteens and the big sacks that contain the bedding rich Indians use on their

144

travels. In the third-class carriages yet more miserable heaps of humanity were piled up, women and children, old men and bare-footed boys. Lying on the luggage-rack, an old man, his black eyes staring out of his head, scratched his head with the stump of his arm. A leper. Immediately beneath him, a woman was feeding a crying infant. The whistle blew; we rushed back to our com-partment. I examined it from floor to ceiling. While I was bend-ing over one of the seats, Aliette screamed. A crouching figure had come out of the lavatory, the "sweeper", an "untouchable". Flourishing a brush and a pan he made it clear that he would travel with us unless he got his baksheesh quickly. Oof! Alone at last!

We locked the doors and shut all the barred windows. There were five alarm signals and a notice in English to the effect that a one-hundred rupee fine would be exacted for improper use. The train jumped along the rails with a deafening racket. Stretched out on the hard, sham-leather seat, I told myself that it was India that was slipping past our padlocked doors; the thought was moving. We slept badly. Every now and then, half waking, I heard a whisper: "Dominique!" "Yes?" "Are you all right?" "Yes." "You're not frightened?" "No."

At dawn a violent push at the door awoke us with a jump. It was the ticket-collector, fresh and spruce as ever, telling us that we were nearly there. A quick wash. The shower did not work well; the basin was not very attractive. The sun was rising, and our single track was running through a stretch of red earth dotted with thick bushes that reminded me of the Mexican desert. The train slowed down and stopped. We had arrived at Bubaneshwar. Heavy-eyed and sour-mouthed, we got out. A lot of little men ran up, offering us their cycle-rickshaws. No use bargaining over the fare; the competition was such that they were ready to accept anything now and would make up for it by arguing later. They could not speak English anyway. It is barely five o'clock and already the air is warm. A red-sanded path led us to the town which was built round a huge, ornamental lake. Women in red saris were washing white linen. Behind the first houses one could espy the carved towers of the temples hidden in their leafy groves. Unbelievers may not enter them. A boy of about twelve, his Brahman cord round his neck, a piece of linen about his waist, offered to be our guide. He spoke a little English, so we agreed.

K

Aliette found him quite lovely. He took us to a smaller lake where the faithful were performing their morning ablutions. Tall women were beating the waters with the corners of their veils, which, being soaked, revealed the whole shape of their bodies. They were really very handsome.

Children were paddling and squealing; old men, their gums blackened by betel, dipped in their cracked big toes whilst streaking their bodies with pink or white lines. A fat man crawled out; the gross folds of his flesh were in great contrast to the thinness of the others. His moustache made him look like an Arab. He approached us, and I asked him if he thought I might photograph the scene. He brushed up his moustache, pushed a forefinger into his ear and said in perfect English: "Here, sir, we are not like Europeans. We do not walk about the beaches in indecent attire. We do not sell photographs of naked women."

He raised his voice and went on more brusquely: "Indians have no share in the sordid hypocrisy that has done so much harm for so many centuries!" And added ironically: "Oh, yes! No doubt you would like to show the beauties of India and of Indian women to your compatriots! I warn you, sir, that if you dare to take a single photograph your camera will instantly be torn to pieces. And you, too, possibly. It would not be the first time I saw such a thing."

Well, that was straightforward anyway!

"We're not English," I said, hoping to placate him. "We're French." Whereupon he flew into a yet greater rage. "That's even worse!" he cried. "India is flooded with pornographic pictures made in France. They show what savages you are!"

No use creating a disturbance; we should certainly have got the worst of it. So we left our xenophobic gentleman and walked on. In some ways these temples would be very like cathedrals were it not for the remarkably erotic nature of some of the carvings. The big temple of Bubaneshwar is of the sixth century. From a near-by platform, one can get a good idea of the monuments it contains. It is less interesting than the older, smaller temples (some of them are of the fourth century) that fill the town with their truncated sugar-loaf domes and are for the most part derelict. Grass and flowers grow about their sculptured walls; men and cows and dogs saunter past. We spent a long time before one very ancient, very lovely temple, enjoying the grace and pro-

fusion of its carvings, the strangeness of the stone animals that
clung to its dome, the Gothic gargoyles and Renaissance scrolls,
the elegance of its shape, the mystery and charm of the thousand
and one figures and tiny elephants that nestled in the mouldings
of its walls.

It was still early—7 o'clock—but the heat was so great that we
thought we would take a rest. We chose the foot of an over-
elaborate obelisk. It stood in a rocky place on the very fringe of
the town; the stone on which we stretched ourselves out had been
worn smooth by time. Just above my head was the rounded rump
of one dancer and the huge breasts of another. Yet some of the
motifs were genuine miniatures, exquisitely carved and let into a
lace-work of red stone. Our search for rest was, however, unsuc-
cessful. Although we seemed hidden, beggars found us out and
drew near, their chests streaked with colours in the traditional
fashion, telling us interminable tales that ended always with the
haunting lament: "Baksheesh! Baksheesh!" They have an innate
gift for comedy and some of their grimaces were very funny.

A sound of voices arose from the path that ran past the temple
towards the town; men were passing by, their skins glistening,
great baskets on their heads. The sound was scarcely more than a
murmur.

The sun shifted and we too had to do so. The heat was really
intolerable; our bad night's sleep made us stupid. A small wind,
heavy, burning, thirst-making, had arisen, and our tea bottles were
empty. The boy-guide, crouching in a corner, was watching us.
We asked him to fetch us some sort of drink, anything provided it
was corked and bubbly. "You know," said Aliette, "the water that
goes fizzzt!" The dangers of ordinary water must be avoided.

Large red ants appeared and made a good meal off our calves.
Judging from the people's thinness, the red ants of India can
seldom have enjoyed such a feast. Aliette sat, barefooted, her
legs crossed, her shirt open, her hair on end and her chin in her
hand, screeching at every bite and watching the men on the
temple path.

"How beautiful they are," she muttered to herself. "Look at
their shoulders, their waists, their lovely slim ankles . . ."

At this point she became silent; a man had just gone by dragging a hideously swollen leg: elephantiasis. We were to see hundreds of cases during our stay, each more monstrous than the last.

The boy came back with a bottle of soda-water. It had no label and tasted warm and rather nasty, but we drank it nevertheless.

It was now midday. The sun was directly overhead and there was no shade anywhere. We were painfully thirsty. A group of cycle-rickshaw men were asleep under a tree. We got hold of two of them and, gesturing freely, asked them to take us to some place where we could drink. They carried us off to a village where we found a shop in which there was a profusion of many-coloured bottles. But we gave up the idea and hurried on towards the station; there was a train to Puri at two o'clock.

The wheels stuck in the sand, the men toiled and struggled so we got out to help them. At last we reached the station tea-kiosk where a stoutish, elderly man was sitting cross-legged and sticking his hairy fingers into a bowl of rice and yellow sauce. We borrowed his saucepan, filled it at a tap marked "Drinking Water", and set it to boil on the charcoal-brazier that was by the kiosk's door. Whereupon, once again we were mobbed by the beggars. Their ways are quite up to date. One of them handed me a piece of paper on which was written, in a clerkly hand: "Dear Sir, Dear Madam. We have been forced to leave our village by the Famine. We are entirely destitute. Please be so kind as to help us."

I threw him a rupee. And instantly regretted it, for at that they all began to quarrel.

The water boiled and we poured it on to the pinches of tea in our bottles. I don't know how many litres we drank under the gaze of the assembled children. They chanted without cease: "Mister! No papa, no mamma, baksheesh, mister!"

The little girls were very pitiful with their great black eyes saddened and ringed with weariness; they were ten years old and looked thirty. One had to hide oneself from the others if one gave them anything. On the platform, the legless, the scrofulous, the sufferers from elephantiasis swarmed. An odour of corruption hung over everything. The train steamed in, and the crowd, which had been prostrate, became alive again. We found a couple of seats in the same carriage as two nuns, who smiled at us most amiably. How could they keep their robes so white in this dust? One of them had rosy cheeks. She managed to make herself heard above the noise of the fans and asked us where we were going and whence we came. She was an Irish missionary. The other was a stout Anglo-Indian who seemed completely case-hardened by much travelling in India.

At every halt people came rushing up to our window, wailing piteously. Hands, arms were thrust between the bars, trying to clutch at our clothes. A horrible stump left a fragment of flesh on the sill. Aliette stifled a cry. The nuns did not blench; no doubt they were accustomed to such scenes.

All along the track were clumps of coconut-trees occasionally overshadowing small huts. In every puddle of water, however black, women were bathing with their swollen-bellied babies.

A few minutes later we arrived at Puri.

33

In Darkest India

MEN in turbans, women in vivid red cotton saris, their arms and ankles bright with heavy silver bracelets, their nostrils inset with precious stones, poured out of our train; Puri is a famous place of pilgrimage.

A cycle-rickshaw carried us over the dunes to a handsome building and a lovely garden full of flowers that filled Aliette with admiration and envy; she was as weary as I of all this discomfort. Unfortunately the cost of the rooms at the B and R Railway Hotel was much too high for us. We had to give up the thought of even the simplest luxury and went to a moderately priced boarding-house. It was an old Colonial-style place, facing the sea. We were greeted by an enormous lady with a wrinkled, highly powdered face and hair done in rolled plaits over her ears. She was completely deaf. We got along, however, with the help of a delightful house-boy, all pointed beard and loud laughter, who made signs at the old girl conveying that we wanted a room.

She replied in a high voice: "I shall be greatly honoured to offer you what you ask for sixteen rupees a day." (A quarter of the Railway Hotel tariff.)

It was certainly a most extraordinary place. Presently the boy reappeared in a white tunic and a turban and ushered us in to dinner. Our hostess beamed upon us. About the room, rather the worse for damp, hung portraits of bearded forebears. The old lady presided at the head of the table. Her son was on her right, a square-faced Englishman with grey hair cut *en brosse*. He bowed very low. On the wall behind him was his engineering diploma from Manchester University. At his right: his sister, a typical old maid in a printed, high-necked, black-buttoned dress. Her eyes were large and blue and she had a velvety mole on her upper lip.

150

The boy served the old lady with much ceremony. She filled her plate and gobbled up her curry greedily. She seemed completely to rule the roost. But she reigned alone. She had lived in this house for fifty years, had not been out of it since the death of her husband, one of the bearded portraits aforesaid. Her daughter did not eat curry and felt the necessity of explaining why, in a slightly precious tone: "It doesn't suit my digestion."

She and I talked. She told me that she had lived here with her mother since her husband (Hullo! I was wrong) died. Every week the post brought her American papers and magazines from the Protestant sect to which she belonged. I asked her: "Are you of Indian nationality?" and she looked very indignant.

"No, sir, I am British."

The brother did nothing all day beyond taking his dog for a walk on the beach. The dog was a mongrel cocker that loved chasing crabs. Its master had views on India and especially on the economic condition of the Indians.

"Just think of it," he said. "If by some miracle, the whole of India were properly worked, if all the goods were taken to the appropriate districts in record time, if not a grain of rice were lost—well! India would still be unable to feed half her population. I lived in Calcutta for a long time . . ."

His face assumed an inspired air.

". . . Do you know that quantities of the grain in the mills are eaten every year by rats? Can you believe that tons of meat rot because there are no trains and no methods of freezing? This country cannot feed its prodigious population, but the worst of it is to see what food there is being wasted by the negligence and indifference of the people who are in charge of it."

The deaf old lady continued to gobble up her food and paid no heed to what was going on about her. Occasionally she broke into the conversation with a few scattered remarks: "Puri is nice —Konarak is better—D'you like Calcutta?"

After dinner we sat on the veranda. The son and his dog disappeared, the daughter retired to her room and her Methodist reviews; the old girl and the houseboy played a game of tiddly-winks. He was a positive virtuoso. It amused him intensely when his opponent, squealing with annoyance, missed the mark.

Puri is a very old and very holy city. Its other name is Jagan-nath, from Jagannatha, "Lord of the World", one of the names of Vishnu. For many long centuries the pilgrims have flocked here to render homage to the god. It is said that the divinity himself built the city; indeed it lives only for him. Puri is not like Benares, a city of many temples; it is an enormous temple that has given birth to a city. The yearly revenue provided by the "demesne of the deity" runs into millions of pounds. It is swollen by the offer-ings of the faithful, which are impossible to calculate but cer-tainly large, although the givers are so poor that their wages are seldom as much as three pounds a month. The god's attendants are divided into thirty-six orders and ninety-seven classes. Below the priests are a host of bakers, cooks, guards, musicians, dancers, singers, torch-bearers, grooms, elephant-keepers, artisans, and furthermore the *mathas,* who, with their servants and their lodgers, are all dependent on the shrine. Not to mention the three thousand "beaters" the temple authorities send round India to drive further pilgrims to the holy place. About twenty thousand men and women and children are directly or indirectly employed by this huge organisation. In a good year the number of pilgrims is about three hundred thousand, of which five-sixths are women. A hundred and forty thousand of them crowd into the city for the Car Festival, the chief of the twenty-four yearly festivals.

A great highway, nearly a hundred yards wide, runs through the town, and it is along this highest of high roads that, in the month of July, the god's great car is drawn amidst the frenzy of his worshippers. It is so heavy that four thousand men, or so I was told, are needed to move it. Beneath its wheels the fanatics used, it is said, to fling themselves, to be crushed and killed for the remission of their sins.

No one but a Hindu is allowed to go into the temple. We had to climb on to the roof of an adjacent house in order to get a clear view of the big twelfth-century enclosure and the lesser concen-tric enclosures within it each containing smaller temples and shrines and crowned, like the shrine at Bubaneshwar, with towers the sculptures of which are even more grossly erotic.

Below us a mass of people whose normal condition would seem to be madness, were passing through the four great portals. Men were suddenly throwing up their arms and shrieking. The April sun was burning hot. What could it then be like in July at the time of the great festival? We descended a staircase that ran through a library where, in dusty glass cases, reposed very ancient documents written on thin sheets of bamboo.

No sooner out of the house than we were encircled by a horde of wild beings who, to attract our attention more certainly and to induce us to give alms with greater generosity, behaved in the most startling manner. One, his hands and feet cruelly shrunken, had had little bells tied on to them and, wriggling on his stomach, jerked himself about, his body twisting this way and that and making a deafening clatter with the bells. Beside him a man hopped about on his one leg; his trouser was torn to expose his mutilation and the tatters of it hung down, flapping like shreds of brown flesh. A third sat motionless, his legs crossed, his body stripped to the waist that we might miss nothing of his skeleton thinness. As in a bad dream we saw other ravaged faces, further tortured frames. The horrible circle barred our way and threatened to press in upon us. Hoping to escape, we produced a few annas and tossed them haphazard. The fleshless hands caught them in mid-air. But other beggars crowded round, attracted by this unusual prodigality, and we had to turn out our pockets and reveal their emptiness before we could get away. Freed at last, we ran off down a side-street, so fast that we almost fell over the worst monster of them all. He was sitting at the foot of a tree; in a low monotonous tone, he was singing. He had no nose; the aperture was so big that we could see the back of his throat. His lips, worn away by leprosy, uncovered a few, betel-blackened teeth; his glance had nothing human in it, a vague glassiness from between swollen and suppurating lids. Seeing us, the nightmare creature made a ghastly grimace that was intended for a smile and held out a hand that was no more than a set of stumps covered with black flies. We dropped a note into it and hurried back. But the horde of beggars had followed us. The man with the withered hands and feet made a frantic noise with his bells; the one-legged man hopped about eagerly. From the monster's inhuman face foam trickled, stained, as though with blood, by betel-juice. He brandished Aliette's note as though to say: "I at least have done well out of my pain!"

The legends of Jagannath's origin go back to the Golden Age, to the far-off days when the King of Malwa sent out Brahmins to seek for the god Vishnu. One of his envoys, Vidyapati by name, travelled through the jungle till he came upon a dwelling where dwelt a solitary worshipper of the god Jagannatha, a pious man who offered flowers and fruit secretly to his lord each day. Vidyapati lodged and became friends with this solitary man and was shown the image of the god: a blue stone resting at the foot of a tree. And one day—according to the tale I was told—as the two were setting their flowers about the stone, a great voice was heard in the jungle saying:

"Good my servants: I am weary of the forest fruit and flowers and would have rice and sweetmeats. You will see me no longer as a blue stone. Henceforth I shall be known as Jagannatha, Lord of the World."

Vidyapati received the revelation with extreme joy and returned to his master to tell him of his discovery. The king promptly summoned all his army and marched with it through the virgin forest. But when he reached the sacred spot the stone had vanished. It had been submerged, the day after the Brahmin's departure, by a sandstorm. The king, in despair, was already doing penance when again a great voice spoke out of the clouds saying that if the penitent offered the necessary sacrifices he would see Vishnu, not in the image of a blue stone but as a mighty tree-trunk. Many signs would accompany the prodigy. The king obeyed the divine command, and the god appeared as a tree-trunk floating on the sea. It came to rest on the beach of Puri at the point where the sacrifices had been performed. The tale goes on to describe how the king gathered together all the carpenters of the land and bade them make of the tree-trunk a statue of the god Jagannatha. But the chisels that the carpenters drove into the wood broke, and the mallets fell awry and bruised the workmen. Whereupon Vishnu, in the guise of a very old woodman, came himself and said that he would carve the image if he were left alone for fifteen days. In this way three idols were made, Jagannatha and his brother and sister. And since that day Jagannatha has been identified with Vishnu, and the faithful have come from all over India to adore him.

Thirty miles or so north of Puri an immense and very ancient temple is sinking finally into the sand. An old motor coach goes there every week, and one morning we decided to travel in it. But the miserable rattle-trap was so overladen and the chauffeur so incompetent that it took us six hours to reach our goal. The chauffeur in question was a Brahmin and little more than a boy; he drove extremely badly. At every pause he cut off his engine which, owing to intestinal trouble, refused to start again. Going through a village we came upon a fakir. He was in a little open booth by the roadside, sitting in the traditional Buddha posture, his legs folded, his body and his head proudly erect, his eyes fixed and unseeing. He was naked, yet wholly coated in dust and cinders. His long, trimmed beard and lovely features made him look like a Christ. Statuesque and beautiful, he remained frozen in this attitude for hours together. So he was on our outward journey; so he was on our return. We saw others, but none were so utterly still. Some held out their hands and spoke to us as we went by. They did not appear to be asking for alms so much as claiming them as a right and they seemed to look upon us compassionately, pitying our ignorance, our foolishness.

The road ran through a forest of coconut-trees and then over a river-bed dried into great patches of cracked earth.

Climbing its bank, our driver, instead of speeding up, put on his brake and changed down into first gear, with the result that we stuck in the sand and had to get down and push. The old bus came out of the ruts inch by inch. Everything about us had been burnt up by the sun, and the people we met looked thinner than ever. Women walked barefoot over the baked fields, great copper jars upon their heads. They were obliged to go like this for miles before they could find any water.

Farther on were little primitive villages where men squatted before their huts, motionless, sunk in apathy, ruminating, maybe, like their even more distressful cattle. They never laughed. Laughter is mostly for full bellies, and theirs were empty. What struck us most was, in fact, the sluggish apathy of these people. We had been told that during the recent famine in Calcutta, whole families died of starvation before shops and restaurants crammed with food. No one thought of throwing a stone through the intervening windows and snatching what was within. You die in India as you walk or breathe. The instinct of self-preservation is so weak that there is even a goddess of smallpox, and leprosy is a sacred thing.

At last we reached Konarak. Not a house, not a living soul

beyond one old man sitting on a stone and selling coconuts. He had a knife with which he made slits in the shells to allow the milk to flow. Beside him a dog with deformed feet dragged its rump painfully over the ground.

But what a glorious sight! In the centre of the huge sand plain stood the Black Pagoda! It used to be so big that its profile could be seen for leagues around, a splendid landmark for sailors on the high seas.

Now it is deserted, and in twenty years' time will have totally vanished, they say, into the sand. It is a sort of pyramid; the apex is rounded and the sides exquisitely carved with thousands of figures of men and beasts, some of which portray every possible attitude of the sexual act with extreme realism. Behind two coco-trees, whose heads nod over the furrowed stones, are two gigantic carved elephants. The entrance itself is preceded by a wide platform adorned with stone cartwheels and divers complicated ornaments.

We sat down, overcome by the lonely splendour before us. Between the feet of an enormous stone horse, whose head and pointed ears tower in the sky, we ate the sandwiches our Puri landlady had prepared for us. The sand was yellow, the trees green, the sky blue, the stone grey and sad. A little child came and sat beside us. His features were quite perfect. He watched us eat with his great black eyes. His beautiful face was thin, his cheek-bones too prominent. We gave him sandwiches, and he took hold of them without saying a word. We continued our walk around the narrow cornices that led us past an incredible number of hidden statues to the top of the temple whence we could see the sea foaming beyond the banana-trees. Returning to our pointed-eared horse, we discovered the sandwiches lying in the sand. The ants were devouring them. For no Brahmin will touch food that has been polluted by the hands of an infidel. We were not surprised. The manservant of the French Vice-Consul in Calcutta had kept everything he ate in a special meat-safe, refusing to use the Frigidaire where the beef and the remains of his master's meals were preserved.

Another six hours of the uncomfortable coach and its decorations which resembled those of a country fair, and we were back in Puri's big high street among the shops that sold bracelets and many-coloured cottons and copper. We were enchanted but exhausted. Our old landlady, still in her sandals, smiled upon us affectionately. We were really glad to be with her again, to be conscious once more of an atmosphere which, however strange to us, was even so less unfamiliar than the Hindu masses. Yet we were becoming accustomed even to these, and it was without any apprehension that we prepared to return to Calcutta.

A good rest, a bathe in the sea of Bengal, and we set out. On the way to the station we stopped in front of a little white stone building surmounted by a tiny black wooden cross. It was the Roman Catholic church. No one visited it but the few nuns scattered about this remote place. The priest was a colossal bearded man in a vast white cassock. He left his native Spain forty years ago to live here alone among people probably the least convertible in the world. He would in all likelihood never go home. His blue Castilian eyes expressed such utter serenity that pity for him faded away.

Next morning we were in Calcutta.

34

The Lepers of Benares

Our trip to the south had dug into our not very considerable capital. Back in Calcutta we were faced once more with the need to earn money. There was only one way: newspaper articles. Luck was with us, and we sold five-hundred-rupees-worth to the *Calcutta Statesman*. From there we went post-haste to the nearest aeroplane company. A Sikh, as charming as he was witty, received us. His wife had just had a baby, he told us, and offered each of us a fine cigar, following a custom that I had supposed was exclusively American. He also allowed us a reduction on the fares to Benares and Delhi.

Next morning, saying farewell to our good friend B . . . . , whose hospitality had been so precious, whose advice so useful, we went off to the Dum-Dum Aerodrome and the DC 3 that carried us away on its coloured wings. The hostess looked like an Andalusian. She was a tall girl with a brilliant complexion. She wore a light, sky-blue sari, and offered us, smiling seductively, chewing-gum, pastilles, sweets of every kind.

The earth was completely dried up; little tufts of greenery surrounded the smallest pool of water; the shadow of the plane glided evenly over the sloping fields.

Benares—a great stretch of land covered with yellow grasses, the customary burst of intense heat as we left the cabin. A group of American tourists was standing by a small building, waiting to take our places. One could not mistake them: tall chaps in multi-coloured shirts, cameras slung round their necks; old ladies in hats and veils, high heels and silk stockings.

"Hullo!" one of them called to me. "All well on board?"

I nodded and asked him what was his particular tour? "Oh!" says he. "We're going round the world in forty-five days."

I registered admiration.

"How did you like Benares?"

"Oh! Benaaaares is grand. Very good food and the hotel is quite comfortable. And you'll see—they've got a beach looks like a million dollars!"

A quarter of an hour later we were in the narrow avenue that led into the town and was much encumbered at the moment with bullock-carts, cycle-rickshaws and tongas. The Hôtel-de-Paris offered itself to us complete with everything the tourist could desire: guides, taxis, snake-charmers—who for a few rupees would show you a mongoose eating a serpent—merchants selling their marvellous, brilliantly coloured saris, some of which were so heavy with gold that they cost a fortune.

In the evening, while the Hindus went to the temples to pray, we wandered up the steep narrow streets. The houses were dullish, mostly ordinary brick. The shops were crammed with brasswork. No doubt the pots were intended for the natives and the statuettes of the gods for the tourists. Sitting on their mats, well-nourished merchants called to us: "Sahib! Memsahib!"

Some even made an effort to get up and show off their wares. Whole cases were filled with gaudy chromolithographs of Vishnu and the terrible Kali or the elephant-headed Ganesh, for whom the Indians have a great liking and whose statues, abominably daubed with red lead, are the only ones that allow strangers to approach them.

A cycle-rickshaw dashed past at full speed, ringing its bell and weaving in and out between the cows that had gathered to eat at a greengrocer's stall. We reached the Golden Temple, the holiest place in this most holy city. The temple is not set in the middle of a square so that one may step back and admire it properly; a tiny alley encloses it, narrow as the Kasbah in Algiers. At every step as one walks around the precincts, one finds people selling flowers or sacred objects, and old, withered-breasted women who stretch out their shrunken arms and murmur prayers. There were now ten, twenty, fifty of them, all sitting in the dust against the walls.

A priest, his fat paunch shining, came up to us and invited us to climb to the top terrace of a neighbouring house. We could not enter the temple, but from up here we were able to see into it. Long-bearded *saddhus*, wrapped in yellowish linen, were rolling on the floor; women were walking tirelessly about a sort of altar on which was a statue; we could not make out its face. At each half-turn the women struck a gong; the sound of it lingered for a long while. Apparently they had to go round seven hundred times, reciting prayers.

They say there are five hundred temples in Benares. From our terrace we could see the domes of a number of them. Before leaving us our priestly guide asked for baksheesh. I gave it to him. He would not accept it, he wanted more! He was so fat as to be obscene. I sent him away. He was, however, most insistent and tenacious, and I had to give him a good hard shove. His greed was as disgusting as the attitude of the poor people was beautiful; poor penniless creatures who deprive themselves of every essential thing they need in order to bring a few flowers to the gods. Almost at every step we came upon a chapel; many of them had been left to decay; their gates were gone. The male and female symbols of generation were so frequent that they became tedious. One saw twenty, thirty phalli covered with dust, worn by time and weather, and then, apropos of nothing, one saw suddenly one that is just like the others but clean, freshly washed in the waters of the Ganges and decked with new-cut flowers. Again, through open doors, we caught sight of the monstrous red or black divinities; Kali with his necklace of human heads, Ganesh whose head is an elephant's.

At sunrise we walked to the Ganges and witnessed a scene of devastating horror and beauty. In the streets that led to the river flowed an endless procession of men, women, and children carrying the vases which they had piously filled with the sacred water and which they covered up in haste as we went by to save them from the pollution of our breath. A man was rolling in a thorn bush. He was as thin as a skeleton and had smears of yellow dust upon his forehead. The thorns covered his naked body, and his bluish flesh was bleeding; beside him black flies swarmed over his excrement. He kept his eyes closed, absorbed in meditation; the passing crowd paid no attention. Farther on women were crouching before the heaps of coloured dust—red, white, yellow—with which the faithful streak their bodies. The effect was very striking. We walked on to the river and reached the top of the great steps. The way was blocked by a number of half-naked lepers, dry-

17. INDIA: Street scene, Benares

16. INDIA: Taxi-rank in Bubaneshwar

19. INDIA: Striking a bargain in a *souk* (native bazaar)

18. INDIA: Benares, the sacred waters of the Ganges

skinned, terribly emaciated, their eyes falling from their sockets and hanging down by the hollow gaps that were their nostrils, covered with flies that they made no attempt to drive away. A fingerless young woman was smoking a cigarette, holding it between the stumps of her hands. Still farther we had a momentary glimpse of a man whose entire face had been devoured by a blood-stained ulcer. Aliette cried out in horror and disgust.

They exhaled an atrocious smell of decay and corruption. A party of cripples shuffled forward. Their legs were bent up beneath them, their heads sunk into their shoulders, their eyes glassy. They descended the steps in little hops and reached the river at the same time as we did. Floating landing-stages had been set up, no more than planks lashed close together and mounted on bamboos. Nobody seemed to notice us; everyone was intent upon accomplishing that task that he wholly believes to be the most important any human being could undertake. Women entered the water. Without thought, young and old revealed the all-too-pitiful secrets of their nakedness. Some indeed were so old and wrinkled that their breasts were like the dugs of aged animals. Under the wet, coloured veils there were sometimes pretty shapes that I looked at with neither embarrassment nor pleasure. Jumping into a boat I let my camera slip out of its case. Fortunately it fell on to a step in shallow water. I snatched it out in great fear lest it should be broken or the film spoilt. O, sacred waters of the Ganges! Not a drop had got in; it never worked better than after its compulsory immersion.

One bank of the river was deserted but the other was a wonderful sight, alive with movement and bright colours and the sound of voices. From our boat, out in the middle of the current, we had a perfect general view of the two sides and the high, white walls of the palaces and the greyish temples, and of the steps and their swarming, many-coloured multitude. A sage, perched on a stone in the Lotus posture, was holding his breath, apparently indefinitely. Higher up, the banks were almost bare again, but as we got nearer to the centre of the town, the steps became more and more crowded and soon there was a dense mass pressing down towards the water, and into the water, under the blazing sun—a mass of white and blue, pink, yellow, red, green, mauve, moving and reflected in the green river, or half-hidden under big straw parasols that cast soft shadows on to the bright waves. Some men

L

walked out waist-deep. They beat the river with their hands and drank of it copiously. On land, the funeral pyres—which are much less impressive than Calcutta's—emitted a fine black soot that fell upon an expanse of drying linen and two copulating donkeys. Benares! We could scarcely believe our eyes.

A strange sight, a sad sight. In some ways it reminded me of the Mexican Indians invading the baroque churches, dragging themselves on their knees from portal to altar, close-packing the walls with ex-votos, sleeping at the foot of crucifixes, making the sign of the cross twenty times running, covering the statues of the saints with kisses. But these wild pagan demonstrations struck me, in the Mexican Indians, not as an empty ritual but as a real faith, personal, simple, passionate. The Hindus swarming by the Ganges did not seem to me so true. They did not pray, and in their presence I could not feel that sense of contact with a deep emotion which the most unbelieving and materialistic of men must feel before a praying figure. I could see no expression in these people's eyes, neither joy nor sorrow nor faith nor love. They were taking part in a purely material ceremony that consisted of certain gestures made in a certain order; wet the body so many times in so many precise places; drink so many mouthfuls of water, throw flowers this way and no other. And were the thunderbolt to fall out of the sky all they could do would be to begin again or somehow come to terms with one of their three hundred million divinities. To be pardoned for the worst of crimes it is not necessary to repent; all one need do is touch the left ear of a Brahmin or bathe in the Ganges in the prescribed order at five prescribed places.

The banks were already quieter; the crowd had stopped filling its brass pots with water and strewing the flowers that float and drift with the current. The lepers were still on the steps of the *ghats*, still rotting in the sun. Aliette shut her eyes and we hurried past. The man in the thorn bush was no longer rolling; he seemed to be asleep. One of the cripples came after us, and we broke into a run. . . . .

We were saturated with this spectacle of wretched, stupefied humanity. Like those Christians who imagine that to find salvation it is enough to go to church every Sunday, these Hindus imagine they can compel their gods to shower blessings in exchange for a ritual in which neither heart nor soul has part.

In the great heat, depressed by what we had seen, all we asked for now was to sit in an air-conditioned drugstore and have one of the best ice-cream sodas in the world. Or to be alone in the shadows and the silence of a cathedral.

35

Hunting the Man-eater

AIR-POCKETS made our journey to the Indian capital uncomfortable. Aliette, always sensitive to changes of pressure, went red, next white, sweated, and sighed at me for reading an Indian magazine. "It's really irritating," she whispered between two ominous hiccups, "the way you never feel anything."

We flew over Lucknow, where the first Indian newspaper was born and where Kipling lived such a long time. Then a vast oasis of foliage and we were in Delhi. A few minutes later a little horse-carriage was taking us through the town. The first impression was excellent; broad avenues, tall trees, circular cross-roads that might be in the bois de Boulogne, bungalows nestling in flowery gardens, long, flat-roofed houses flying the flags of every imaginable country, sumptuous cars, new, yellow-painted buildings; for the moment the India of poverty and pain had vanished.

We called upon the French Ambassador, Count O...., a cultured, distinguished-looking man with a charmingly simple manner. He invited us to the dinner he was giving that evening for the Indonesian Ambassador who was just off to France. Dinner jacket and long dresses of course. In New Delhi you dress at evening. The best society congregates there.

The Vice-Consul at Calcutta had given us a letter of introduction to Henri D...., Delhi's Second Secretary. We took it to him. A tall young man, his hair cut *en brosse*, he received us in his small, well-ventilated office. "The Ambassador has just told me that he has invited you to dinner tonight. That's good. And I would be very glad to put you up. That is," he added, laughing, "if you have nowhere better to go."

We were touched by such a greeting.

164

"Unfortunately," he went on, "I shan't be able to show you round. I and my wife are hunting tigers next week in Rajasthan."

I felt myself going pale at the thought. I couldn't help exclaiming: "You *are* lucky!" and even added, in defiance of the most elementary good manners: "It's my pet ambition—to hunt tigers."

Aliette gave me a furious look. A scene in the offing.

But D . . . . only smiled and said: "Listen. You seem so keen I'll send a wire to the Maharajah asking if we can bring two friends."

I collapsed into my chair with joy. Aliette, very stiff and cold, said nothing. We thanked D . . . . effusively and left.

In the passage Aliette let me have it: "Well, of all the infernal cheek!"

"I know," I said humbly, "but I did want to go so much."

"That's no reason for behaving like a guttersnipe!"

"Thank you. Is that all? I suppose that *you* who have been brought up so beautifully—*you* won't have anything to do with my beastly bad manners—*you* won't come with us to hunt tigers?"

"Since it's all fixed I wouldn't be such a fool as to miss the chance."

The argument broke off at this point. There were more pressing things to see to. Aliette had sent her evening dresses back to Paris. She had to get hold of one immediately. So we dashed off to Old Delhi to try to find a bit of stuff that she could wear. Up and down the bazaar we went, compelling poor devils of merchants to undo every roll in their shops. Aliette soon infected them with a feverish agitation increased by cries of, "No, not that one." "Yes, over there. No, just behind. Yes." "No, it's hideous." "Oh! that's perfect!" Finally we chose a big piece of green sari patterned in brown. Aliette draped it this way and that, blinked, bent, pinched and folded the stuff in a thousand different fashions. I gave the merchant six rupees, which he slipped one by one into the fold of his shirt, staring at us in amazement.

While Aliette went off to find a tailor to hem her stuff, I ran to Connaught Place to buy a black bow-tie. I had lost mine in Bangkok. But no! I went into twenty of the smartest shops but they had only ready-made ties. I finished by getting a shocker that would certainly make my wife say yet again that however hard I tried I could never be just "right".

As for her, under the chandeliers of the Embassy's grand dining-room, among the women in their best clothes and the exquisite servants in white cockaded turbans, she looked, in her six-rupee green sari, quite dazzling.

The Maharajah had cabled that he would be "delighted to see us", and a couple of days later, at dawn, we started off with M. and Mme D .... and took our places in an air-conditioned carriage, "Made in Switzerland", of the Bombay express. The seats were upholstered in pale blue leather. We were deliciously comfortable. A tall and turbaned Sikh came every now and then to see that we had all we wanted. We were in another world from the parched landscape that glided past the double windows and from the packed crowds milling on the station platforms. A little after noon we arrived at a small town, Kotah, in the heart of Rajasthan. One of the Prince's aides had come to fetch us in a superb Chevrolet. Getting out of the train we stepped from a temperature of about 68 degrees to one of 120. It made our heads reel.

On each side of the rough road the rocky ground extended as far as the eye could see, sprinkled with clumps of leafless bushes. It was much encumbered by bullock-carts that swayed and zig-zagged from right to left. But presently, upon a hill upon which clustered a confusion of white houses, there rose, beyond a high wall with many delicately carved turrets, the old palace of the Rajah of Bundi. It was half-deserted; the Prince no longer lived there. His new palace was on the other side of the white houses and the steep streets that made the town look so strangely Italian. The women wore long, full skirts falling in folds about their heavy, carved silver anklets. They carried jars on their heads and walked in small groups, very erect, very proud, bringing water from the well to their encampment. They belonged to a tribe of nomads which roams from town to town in little two-wheeled carts that have great nails to ornament their sides and a shape that reminds one of the winged chariots of ancient mythology.

Crouching beside the wheels of these carts were other women feeding a fire. They drew their veils over their faces as we drove by, or lowered their great dark eyes. The men were in bright red or ochre turbans; they gave us a dull stare.

A hairpin bend, a troop of monkeys that went leaping across the road, and suddenly two sentinels who presented arms. The palace was a long, white, crenellated building. We passed under a vast porch, went round a huge pool on which ducks floated, turned to the right and stopped under a smaller porch supported by elegant pillars. Three servants ran to collect our luggage, and the aide, a pleasant, plumpish gentleman, conducted us to our rooms. We passed through a vast hall adorned with tigers' and buffaloes' heads and then through a wide corridor that led to a courtyard and a softly playing fountain. The courtyard was divided into a set of square lawns enclosed on two sides by long, white, crenellated walls. Before us a two-storeyed façade; a flagstaff which flew the Maharajah's colours. There was not a breath of wind in the clear, blue sky. The left-hand façade was pierced by an oval of small peep-holes. Behind it were the apartments of the Maharanee, the Prince's wife, whom only Aliette and Mme D. . . . might visit. Another corridor, and we passed under a gallery that looked out on to the ornamental pool we had caught sight of so recently. A number of wooden doors. The aide opened one of them, and, Behold! an immense room, two beds, a desk, voluptuous arm-chairs, cupboards—our room. Next door there was a pink marble bathroom and a little boudoir. White-coated menservants brought us tea, cakes, iced drinks and cigaretes. Aliette gazed about her happily and made a dash for the bathroom and the shower.

Dinner was at midnight and luncheon at four in the afternoon. Towards evening we went out on to the lawns. Rocking-chairs and deck-chairs awaited us; lemon-squashes, cocktails and whiskies were served. The Prince's Chamberlain appeared and welcomed us. He said that the Prince would be down in a moment. He was an Englishman, not very thin, and almost bald as to the head. Monkeys were jumping over the roofs. Sometimes they stopped suddenly, gave us a sharp look, scratched themselves, let out a shriek and vanished. The Chamberlain pointed to the wall and said in a fat voice, "Do you know that the wife of the Belgian Counsellor shot a panther there last week?"

He rose to his feet; the Maharajah had joined us. He was quite young, and was dressed in grey linen trousers, a printed shirt—its sleeves rolled up—and a very small scarf. "Hullo! Hullo!" he said, shaking us cordially by the hand. "How nice of you to come."

The day was ending; the crenellations grew sharp against the bright, clear sky, the moon rose, and a delicious freshness added to our well-being. Towards eleven, we all went to our rooms and put on bathing-dresses. His Highness dived from a first-floor window into the ornamental pool, among the sleeping ducks. The water was exquisitely cool and we swam to a little temple that was in the middle of the pond. Dinner, which we ate in full evening dress, was served on one of the square lawns of the courtyard, which was purposely floodlit. A dozen orange-turbaned servants were busy about the table and its shining glass-ware.

A vision of fairyland. Once again, in this Arabian Night's palace, we could but forget, for a while, the murmur of India's suffering millions.

As soon as the meal was over, the Maharajah invited us to track down some of the wild animals that were to be found near the palace. Aliette's eyes shone. We changed our clothes quickly and met the others by the central porch. His Highness drove his own hunting-jeep, an astonishing machine, bristling with firearms and searchlights. The windscreen had been lowered, and a number of heavy rifles were propped against it. Very exciting. The jeep bowled slowly along; the searchlights raked the undergrowth. A pause: a few dozen yards ahead of us two green eyes glowed in the night.

"What is it?" Aliette asked in a low voice.

The dazzled creature remained quite still; other eyes lighted up so that the bush became a strange spray of luminous points.

"Those are blue bulls, nylghau," the Maharajah whispered back. "We shall get near to them presently."

We drove quietly on. From time to time a cart, lit by a lantern, met us on the path. The driver was chanting monotonously to himself to keep his nerves steady; the place was full of wild beasts. The jeep went faster, slower, proceeded along a hollow way that led to a small lake. The full moon shone with such brilliance that we needed no searchlights to enjoy the astonishing sight of gazelles drinking. The creatures moved with their heads erect, stopped, listened, trotted a little way. Farther on a pack of jackals were finishing, gluttonous and silent, their meal of camel's carcass. An enormous porcupine, bigger than any to be seen in Europe, ran swiftly off at our approach.

"It is a very dangerous animal," the Maharajah warned us." Its spines are poisonous and the wounds they inflict are almost always fatal."

Two little eyes in the brush; a fox. "Pooh!" snorted Aliette contemptuously.

Our host had the most remarkable eyesight and was completely used to hunting by night. He often slowed down, catching sight, no doubt, of an animal that I looked for vainly in the swivelling beams of the searchlights.

Hup! Stop! Two eyes, apparently, were shining on our right. It took me quite a few seconds to see them. We bumped over the uneven ground as the big beasts galloped off. The blue bulls. The Maharajah changed gear, increased his speed. We clung tightly to our seats so as not to be thrown out. The jeep leant sideways, swung round, bounced, landed again. The bulls continued to gallop ahead, and we pursued them at about forty miles an hour over bush and field and ditch. They looked like monsters, bolting, distracted, in every direction, kicking the lumpy earth behind them into clouds of dust.

On the way back, His Highness suddenly stopped, cut out his motor and signed to us to be absolutely still. Our lamps shone on a thick copse, Close to the ground, about a hundred yards away, were two round, green eyes. It was most impressive. The field-glasses passed from hand to hand and presently, in the massed beams I discerned a big head. I could see no details. From a ditch, a cicada filled the night with its harsh creaking. Aliette wriggled in her seat; we were all terribly excited. The Maharajah got out, moving soundlessly; he put up his glasses and whispered very low, "A panther." It took my breath away. It would have been suicide to approach the beast on foot, and the copse was so thick that the jeep could not pass through it. The Maharajah picked up a gun. He was going to fire, but only to frighten. Since he could not pursue and kill it, he did not want it to be wounded—a wounded panther is very dangerous. He fired. In a crackling of branches, the panther leapt and vanished.

A few moments later His Highness was giving the password to his sentinels and we were in the palace grounds again.

The perfect *dolce far niente*. . . . Large breakfasts served in bed, swimming in the pool, riding out over the countryside and, in my case, the discovery of the skeleton of the dead camel still haunted by circling vultures. We had been told in confidence that there was a tiger in the neighbourhood, but the palace trackers had to find out his exact position. Lying in a rocking-chair, I was waiting for Aliette. She had been to pay her visit to the Maharanee in her cloistered apartments behind the pierced wall. Presently she came to me, highly excited, and told me all about it.

"Unbelievable! Unbelievable!" she cried. "Just imagine. I went up a narrow staircase into a room papered in the most ghastly pink. The Maharanee was expecting me. And what do I see? I shapeless *lump* of a woman, absolutely round, lost in fat! And they say she is only twenty-seven! Utterly incredible! She smiled at me in a sad, shy sort of way, holding up the corner of her sari. Another ghastly pink! I had been told that that was her only colour. She wears a little diamond in her nostril.

"I asked her what she did all day. She told me she just ate! She said it in quite a nice, soft voice. I'd been told too that she only talked about her stomach-aches and her dog's stomach-aches. Not a very hopeful start for a conversation, you must admit! What would you say to a woman who never goes out and knows nothing of our amusements or our worries? I asked about her children. They're at a boarding-school near Delhi. That seemed to please her and she began to talk about them in her little soft voice. And in perfectly good English.

"She told me her daughter was eight years old, and brought out a photograph from under her veil. 'She's changed a lot,' she said, 'since this was taken. I've often asked her for another but nobody will give me one...' And then she stopped and hesitated and asked me very shyly if I could get her another photograph. 'It would give me so much pleasure,' she said.

"Her stress on the word 'pleasure' was pathetic. It must be her only small joy in life. She has a son but seldom sees him. And the Chamberlain told me that her daughter had said once, 'It's a bore being with Mamma, she's so uneducated. She really ought to try to learn.'

"Don't you think that's awfully sad?

"Anyway she does eat! All the time I was there she never stopped nibbling nuts or sweets of sorts. They were spread out in front of her on a large tray.

"I really didn't know what to say. In despair I asked her very respectfully if I might see her jewels. The idea seemed to tire her extremely, but she was full of good will and called one of her many women servants and presently a girl appeared, barefoot, in the doorway and then came back with her arms full of jewel cases.

"You can't imagine how thrilled I was! Emerald necklaces and ruby necklaces and diamonds and pearls! And everything mounted on solid gold with lovely enamel patterns on the back so that you can wear it inside out. I don't know how many necklaces she showed me and bracelets and anklets and earrings and diamonds and rings for the nose and brooches. At least a hundred.

"She only puts on these marvellous things at religious ceremonies and anniversaries. That is about three or four times a year.

"'And when I do wear them,' she said. 'I have to wear the whole set—jewels on the head and in the nose and on the arms and the ankles—it's terribly heavy!'

"I got quite depressed thinking of all that stuff sitting in its cases. She told me she had lots more at the old palace.

"Do you realise that this woman never goes out? Occasionally she is carried off to Bundi in a carriage that has thick curtains so that no man shall ever see her.

"She noticed that I was sorry for her—for being so definitely sequestered, you know. 'I was brought up to it,' she said.

"And such a healthy life! Eating till you're sick, never seeing a soul, never moving. It gives me the shivers just to think of it. She was very sweet to me, but *what* a life!"

One morning the Maharajah came to see us and to announce, with a flash of the eyes, that a tiger had carried off a cow in the village, had wounded a man and was back in his lair. The road to it was long and difficult; we were to start at once.

What did that matter? We jumped for joy, and got ready double quick. A big green station-wagon took us over the dusty road. It felt as though we were off on a punitive expedition. The three aides were there in their topees, their rifles between their knees. They had driven tanks in the war; during the Burma campaign one of them had been wounded in the actual tank commanded by the Maharajah. The windows were all shut; the wind was burning hot.

We stopped on the bank of a dried-up river where a lorry awaited us and several jeeps for the uniformed trackers and the beaters. The latter were barefooted and naked to the waist and armed with little hatchets. His Highness, in a wide felt hat that had a green ribbon about the crown and was adorned with a pink feather, was making out his plan of operations with his staff. In Indian file, trackers and beaters ahead, we started to walk along the dry nullah, then through the leafless, grey and yellow undergrowth. Sinking into the sand, burnt by the sun, parched by the dust, we made slow progress. The line became considerably stretched out. Aliette flushed, her feet were swollen, she began to lag behind, to breathe with difficulty. A gallant aide held her up so that she did not fall. She muttered to herself, "Lord! One must really *want* to hunt tigers."

Coveys of partridges took flight at our approach and deer bolted into the scrub. The beaters tramped easily on, and not a drop of sweat sullied their smooth brown skins. Poor us! We were melting. Aliette was a pitiful sight. We got past thorn-bushes that were blue and frequented by beautiful birds of many colours. In the ponds that the sun had not yet sucked up, flamingoes lifted their long legs, stepping lightly, like conspirators. At times we came upon a hamlet surrounded by mud walls or thorn hedges. Saris were hanging up to dry upon strings—blue, red, yellow, green, white—and fluttering in each breath of wind like banners.

At one of the huts the women waved their bejewelled arms and made a great fuss of us. It was in their compound that the tiger had killed the cow that morning and wounded the man. Just beyond, one almost obliterated trail crossed another. We stopped and were told to keep our voices low; the man-eater was lying up in a cleft of the hill ahead of us, a hundred yards or so away. The Maharajah, leaning on his gold-pommelled sword-stick, was conferring secretly with his trackers. Collapsed on the ground, we were drinking every drop from the gourds which the aides handed us and seeking in vain for the shade of a thorn-bush. (On our return we discovered where the water came from and promptly resigned ourselves to contracting every dire disease.) The beaters sat on their heels in a circle round us; they eyed our sorry looks with a certain curiosity. Their fresh, alert appearance was positively insulting. I did not hesitate to lie down and was brutally called to order by Aliette, who considered that such conduct in front of natives was really too undignified. For her part she was

examining and fingering the blisters on her feet. Both my handkerchiefs, soaked in eau-de-cologne, were being used as padding
for her American moccasin shoes.

His Highness had finished his conference by now, and we were
separated into two groups; Mrs D . . . . , an aide and our host on
the one hand, Aliette, Henri D . . . . and myself on the other. The
three of us went up to a little stunted tree that had a mat spread
over it, forming a sort of narrow platform. There was a shaky,
improvised ladder. Aliette climbed up it first, tried to balance on
the platform, could not manage it, tried again, spun round and
ended up between two branches. The tree creaked and groaned
in a most sinister fashion. Henri went up next, and I followed him.
I suddenly remembered reading somewhere that the most dangerous thing in a tiger hunt was to break an arm or a leg. I must say
the way our perch swayed and creaked was not at all reassuring;
it was so dried up that perhaps it was already dead. Henri was
the only one of us who had a rifle and he confessed humbly that
he had never attacked anything fiercer than the rabbits of
Sologne. The best I could do, my camera on my chest, my
legs swinging in the void, was to keep as well balanced as I
could. A couple of hundred yards away the other three were
climbing into a *machan* from which they might be able to shoot
the tiger.

Long silences, broken at times by a little cry from Aliette who
was in constant danger of falling. The beaters, bent double,
hatchet in hand, went forward methodically surrounding the cave
in which the wild beast was hiding. A smell of dry leaves, of burnt
bark, of hot sand. . . . Suddenly two far-off calls on a whistle, and
the most deafening noise broke out, explosions, yells, tom-toms—
the whole countryside was full of it. The beaters threw stones into
the cave, and the huge beast bounded forth. He sprang at a man,
who was saved only by a prodigious jump into a tree. The tiger
roared loudly, harshly, furiously. Cold sweat ran down my back.
His long tail erect, he looked about him and roared again. Men
shouted and threw stones. The tiger leapt forward, breaking
branches, crushing one bush, jumping on another, rushing straight
down the corridor that separated us from the Maharajah. Wonderful to see the enormous creature, alarmed yet full of fight. A
report. The tiger rolled over, snarling horribly, but was up at
once, saw the Maharajah and went for his tree. Another report.

Again the beast rolled over, arose and, with magnificent courage, made for his enemy. But by now a crimson stain was spreading over his shoulder. Once more he charged, still roaring hideously. Another shot rang out, and he reared, fell, struggled, dragged himself a little way and rolled over, mortally hurt.

A prolonged whistle proclaimed the death of our Lord Man-eater. A smell of gunpowder, of sweat, of blood. Clinging to the main branch of our tree, we had followed the scene with agonised attention. One more report shook the heated air, and cries of joy were heard around; women came running from nowhere and everywhere and started to sing. All the villagers had assembled to see the dead tiger slung between two long poles and borne away by four half-naked men. The great tail swept the ground, the head swung sadly in the dust of the carriers' feet. The village women, brilliantly bedecked, walked elbow to elbow, clapping their hands and yelling with joy. I had a strong feeling that in some of the ecstatic hymns they were singing in their hard, raucous voices were verses addressed to us, for the men, as they passed by, still carrying their hatchets, glanced in our direction and smiled knowingly.

The procession stopped at the hamlet. The heat was so great that the tiger had to be gutted at once. The flies were already buzzing round the entrails that fell out of its wounds and smelt abominably.

Then came the solemn moment when the cameras were called upon to record, to immortalise, the end of this princely hunt. Mine did not function; the film was too old.

And so we returned over the arid, stony ground, past the yellow thorn-bushes. Aliette's feet were swelling again and she hobbled painfully along. ADCs were on either side of her; she clung to their arms. I could see the road in the distance, a haven in the desert, and presently we reached it and found a sumptuous meal, laid out by numberless menservants under a big tree, on a magnificent Persian carpet. Iced beer, junket, all sorts of meat dishes, jars of Russian salad, plates of bread and biscuits, quantities of cakes. Was it all a mirage? The feast reconciled us to the cruelties of Nature and the chase. I drank twelve tankards of beer straight off.

At midnight, after the cannon's traditional salute, we were back in our white ducks and long skirts, dining in the floodlights.

Before we left, the Maharajah presented us with a signed photograph of himself framed in dark wood and bearing his crest. We were to meet him again in Europe. He goes there every summer, leaving a steward to take charge of his palace, his horses, his eighteen cars and his hundred and twenty-five servants.

36

A Difficult Journey to Pakistan

Now for Pakistan. No hope of a lift in a car, so there was only one way, the train. On inquiry we found that no trains go direct to Pakistan. The Frontier Mail stops at Amritsar. After that one has to take a motor-coach to the no-man's-land that separates India from Pakistan and another coach on. The information we were given was rather vague; no one goes by this train and bus route that we, for economy's sake and for the sake of adventure, proposed to adopt.

On the evening of our departure, storm descended upon the capital of India. Spinning columns of sand raced down the streets at an incredible speed and cars scraped blindly past each other. Dust was everywhere. In a few seconds, in the taxi that was taking us slowly to the station, we were white with it and our teeth were full of grit. The station itself was a fantastic sight. Eddies of transparent dust moved across it; the veils of the saris billowed out at each gust; among the women, hurrying back and forth in their bright draperies, and the halt and the maimed, children sat on their luggage and wept. Boys passed by in procession bearing great bundles on their heads like porters in the jungle. A stupefied cow relieved itself in the middle of the hall and then ambled off to eat the vegetables that were sticking out of a crate.

A kindly, immensely tall Sikh had been given charge of us. He fulfilled his mission eagerly and pleasantly. During the journey he told us something of his own life. A refugee from Pakistan, he lived with his wife and six children in one room in Old Delhi. He

176

20. AFGHANISTAN: The silversmiths heat up their fires

21. AFGHANISTAN: A typical
    inhabitant

22. IRAN: One of the mosques of Ispahan

23. IRAN: Street scene, Zahidan

had only been working on the railway for six months and earned
seventy rupees (that is about £4) a month. We couldn't quite
make out what his friendliness really portended: the wish for a
tip or merely the desire to confide his troubles?

At dawn, we noticed large posters in Arabic lettering on the
walls of the Amritsar suburbs. It was seven o'clock and we had
to sit for two hours in the waiting-room before we could get to a
bank and change our money. Our Sikh came over to us every now
and then, ready, it seemed, to satisfy our slightest whim.

Amritsar is the home of the Sikhs. They formed a Hindu sect in
the sixteenth century but have been much influenced by Moham-
medanism. They do not recognise caste, do not employ Brahmins
in the ceremonies and have no idols. Actually they have adopted
the laws of several religions; they still allow the sacred cows to
wander where they will, after the Hindu fashion, and they burn
their dead. They do not smoke, but they do drink, and have
invented a tale to justify this licence. "Once upon a time a holy
man saw two doves drinking water. Having drunk, they fought to
the death. So the holy man bade his people put sugar in the
water." The Sikhs obeyed with alacrity and, stretching a point,
allowed the juice of the sugar-cane to ferment, thus producing
alcohol.

Nine o'clock struck. The station, which is the rail-head for all
India, was teeming with men, their beards rolled round a thread,
and women in baggy trousers. Having piled our luggage on a
small horse-cart, we went to the Imperial Bank of India where a
big, red-haired, freckled and tortoiseshell-spectacled Englishman
received us. Such men are still, though rarely, to be met in India,
their imposing bulk comfortably installed in red leather arm-
chairs and towering above the rickety chairs of their exasperat-
ingly slow and disgustingly wretched-looking Indian subordinates.

Our Sikh then led us through many twisting and evil-smelling
alleys to a sort of metal lorry, painted blue, that was already surrounded by travellers and the inevitable beggars displaying their
infirmities. We sat down on a milestone and waited for the thing
to start. Our big Mexican hats caused a sensation; the crowd
gathered about us in a compact mass. The motor coughed; the
driver installed himself in his seat; he was wearing sun-glasses.
We climbed in, having said good-bye to our companion, who was
almost in tears between his farewells and his gratitude. I mopped

M

my forehead; Aliette made up her face. Through the noise of the motor I shouted at her:

"All right?"

"Yes. What about you?"

"Not too bad."

"What heat!"

"I'm depressed."

"Why?"

"What a country!"

"Yes."

"You would never care to go back?"

Her answer was almost lost in a gruesome cracking sound. It seemed as though the motor-coach-lorry was about to fall to pieces.

"The men are so beautiful . . ."

"But the country disappointed you?"

"Yes, I suppose so. I mean I suppose I expected something more. I don't know what. Something I got out of books or my own imagination. But it is an extraordinary, strange, mysterious country all the same."

"I'm disappointed, too. I had hoped to find sages and philosophers, the men our professors at school used to say were the representatives of the genuine and constructive element in humanity. I don't know, but I should say the Indians are the opposite of the future. They are a primitive people who can't stand up to things. Their religion takes away all wish for action."

"No," said Aliette. "You're exaggerating as usual. I may have been disappointed but I don't feel they are as spineless as you think. What we saw at Benares doesn't seem to me much different from what you see at Lourdes and such places. The good ladies who burn candles in our churches hoping for this or that advantage look to me just as half-witted as the Hindu women floating little lights on the sacred Ganges. All that is just superstition, and you will find superstition everywhere."

"You may be right, but don't the feelings you bring to a ritual count at all? I'm not speaking of the seers and sages of the Upanishads, but surely the ordinary people you see everywhere—have they the faintest sense of love and faith when they pray? After all their religion is a religion of terror. You've only to look at their gods."

"Perhaps so," Aliette answered, "but we are taught too that we shall burn in hell if we wander from the straight and narrow path and that the fear of God is the gift of the Holy Spirit. All religions are alike. . . ."

The conversation was beginning to wander. I really did not know what to say, so changed the subject:

"Personally I think that the test of civilisation is how women are treated. Think of the little girls who are married at twelve and the widows who are still accursed today and who, only a short time ago, had to throw themselves into the fire and be burnt with their dead husbands or be damned for ever. The Indian woman is the lowest form of slave. That is not a sign of a great civilisation."

Our conversation ended. My neighbour bared a withered breast from her sari and started to feed her naked baby. The child sucked greedily; its bony legs were half on my knees. Aliette fingered our typewriter anxiously. It was under the seat and emitting odd noises. At last we reached a wooden hut and the coach stopped; the new Indian frontier was only a few yards away. A fat, smiling individual, accompanied by two big Sikhs in olive turbans, watched us alight and roared with laughter at our Mexican hats. He shook us by the hand and led us to the guard-room. Other Sikhs were there, combing their long hair. Aliette was much amused; her own first impulse on arriving in any town is to go and get her hair done. Visas and Customs, all the various formalities were gone through in a perfectly friendly atmosphere.

Good-bye India! But Pakistan does not begin on the other side of the fence. We had to go on foot across nearly two miles of no-man's-land. Aliette swore under her breath; I could see from her face just how she felt about our little walk. Moreover it was noon and the Custom House thermometer registered a hundred and thirty in the shade. . . .

"Left, right, left, right!" But my wife at the moment was in no mood for humour. We had to stop and rest; the sweat poured into my eyes and made them smart; Aliette was as red as a lobster; no doubt some of the colour was due to bad temper.

It took us a longish while to get from India to Pakistan, those hostile brothers. Our hands were torn by the handles of our infernal bags. But a white crescent on a green flag was waving from a mast-head behind a sentry-box, and at last we sank down on our bags, puffing like grampuses, to watch the peculiar and comic ceremony of the changing of the guard. Four men in khaki linen, berets perched over their ears, their faces ill-shaven and dirty, were performing under the orders of an officer so fat that his belt and shoulder-strap could scarcely meet over his navel. He held himself very erect, his swagger-stick under his arm, his hairy calves swelling below his shapeless shorts.

"Oooooh! Poom-patapoom!"

Clicking of heels, right turn, more heel-clicking, faces front, half-turn left, click again.

The four soldiers repeat the exercise, putting in a few extra clicks, a step forward, a step back, two to the side, a half-turn right, rat-tat-tat on the ground, more steps forward, half-turn left and "left, right, left, right"—good-bye. The scene lasted quite a quarter of an hour, and all for what? To deposit a poor chap in a hut to examine our passports. He savaged them with his great grubby fingers, held them upside down and only got them straight when he came to the photographs. At these he had a good look. Needless to say, he could not read. Yet finally he stiffened into a salute and made a sign with his head that we might proceed.

Next we were confronted by a sort of big barn, three old chairs, and a desk covered with papers on which an unwashed gentleman had laid his head and was sleeping soundly.

He awoke. His shirt was hanging out of his trousers. He rubbed his eyes and, reaching instinctively for a pen, copied a page of our passports into a dog-eared register. The nib had lost one of its points and squeaked. Having made this effort the gentleman went to sleep again, and we struggled on to a pisé building, presumably the Customs. Nobody! We hunted round for a sign of life and finally discovered six young men asleep in a garden. We gave one of them a gentle shake, which caused him to awake and lead us to a large room and a white wood table where he sat down, and more scribbling in registers followed. A boy brought us tea, which we drank gratefully. The clerk watched us with a bleary eye and let us go without so much as a glance at our luggage.

An hour's wait, sitting on the baking ground. The sound of a motor roused us from our coma, for this was surely the Lahore coach. Wonder of wonders, it was a magnificent affair, brand new, with a top deck such as you see in the streets of London! We could hardly believe our eyes. Aliette, revived by the prospect of a little ease, walked towards it briskly. We took a front seat on the green leather cushions beneath a "Made in England" clock bearing the arms of the City of London. Our hopes of relative comfort were nevertheless dashed; the coach was soon full to bursting point with a cargo of dirty, noisy, strong-smelling humanity. On a seat next to ours a woman was holding a bundle on her knees, wrapped in the corner of her sari. A violent jolt uncovered a baby that was all skin and bone with a horribly distended belly and a sweating face. The mother covered it up again quickly. Under the veil the child lay still, yet we could make out its rapid breathing. The mother appeared totally indifferent.

"It's going to die," Aliette whispered in alarm.

Outside the long windows the desert slipped past and an occasional camel. The child's breathing became yet shorter and faster; the sweat had soaked through the veil so that its body was clearly outlined.

"How awful," Aliette said, "to think that someone is dying beside you and you can't do a thing." She looked furiously at the woman, who lazily waved a fly away from her face.

The veil jerked up and down. The conductor, bland and fat of face, pushed his way through the chattering people. A woman drew her sari over her naked breast. A flight of ravens arose from off the road and flapped away clumsily on black wings.

By now, under the veil, the gasping breath had become faster and faster. A ghastly obsession . . . and then, while the driver avoided a cow and the woman flicked off another fly, there was suddenly quiet. Appalled, we stared at the bundle that lay so still. The child was dead.

The ochre walls of Lahore were on either side, covered with advertisements of the Bata factory. The coach stopped before the station. We carried our bags to the cloakroom but the man refused at first to take them "because they are not locked". Cheerful thought! He yielded presently, under baksheesh pressure, but still without giving us a guarantee.

We were told that the train for Peshawar would not come through for twenty-four hours and that as it started from Karachi one could not reserve seats at Lahore. This was the last straw, and for the moment we were utterly crushed. The time was four in the afternoon; we had eaten practically nothing since last night. Aliette sank, exhausted, on a bench.

"Dominique, you can do what you like, I'm finished. I shall stay here."

"Come on! Try! Let's go to the station office. We may be able to book seats."

She made a furious gesture and retorted:

"*You*, of course, are perfectly happy. The more trouble the better! But I'm tired of travelling this way. I'm hungry, I'm thirsty, I'm dead beat. You don't understand! You force me to do things no woman would think of doing. Look at me! I'm disgusting! I'm repulsive!"

Aliette's supreme argument! Her first concern on arriving anywhere is to fly to a shower and wash. How often have I been called a "dirty beast" because I have not found out instantly whether all conveniences were in working order!

I sat down beside her and said affectionately:

"Listen. You're not being fair. I don't think we've done so badly so far. We've travelled on some of the best boats, we've stayed in palaces——"

She interrupted me. "Am I complaining? All I say is that I can't go any farther till I've washed. You're impossible! You don't care! Just push on however one is, dirty or clean. One tries a place and if it's too dear one bargains or one tries another."

It is true that in the excitement of the moment I do sometimes forget I have married a fashion editress.

All the same, a quarter of an hour later, we were in the booking-office. But the man was adamant; we could not reserve seats. A nasty blow. What could we do? Aliette, who had not opened her mouth, glanced at me wearily.

We could but try elsewhere. My wife, dragging her feet, followed me at a distance of twenty paces. Breakers ahead! I should have to do something about it quickly. To quieten Aliette I ought to have looked at once for a restaurant where we could eat and wash, but, as usual, I could not rest until I had made sure of the next move. No doubt I *am* a monster of selfishness. It is this very lack of consideration that Aliette was blaming me for. However, we reached a square where a big building, the Orient Airways, stood. I went into a large, shadowy room, and my wife, following me, collapsed into the nearest arm-chair.

"I want to talk to the manager," I said to a tall gentleman in white.

"I am the manager."

I told him our story, to which he listened with every show of interest. At the end of it he smiled, reflected for a moment, and then said:

"I can give you fifty per cent off the fares to Peshawar. But the next plane starts the day after tomorrow."

I looked up at the ceiling and made a quick calculation. Fifty per cent of the fares to pay and three days in a hotel. Impossible; we had not got the money.

"Sorry: I am most grateful but we can't afford it."

"Wait a minute," the man said. "Perhaps it can be managed. I will ring up the head office at Karachi and see if they will take you free."

He lifted the receiver. Aliette was dozing in her corner. I woke her up and told her I had some hope. "All right, all right," she muttered.

It was no use waiting for the result of the call. We set out to look for lunch in Lahore's main avenue. We could see white houses and presently a kind of tea-shop served by a number of turbanless men.

The cashier was an enormous Anglo-Pakistani. She lifted her nose from her accounts and gave us a "Good afternoon" worthy of Regent Street. Aliette rushed off to wash her hands and face. Returning, she seemed calmer. She chose an imposing plateful of good-looking cakes, ordered iced coffee. It distressed her that I would not eat also. I confessed that I simply couldn't; my stomach was in knots, waiting for the Orient Airways' answer.

The cashier handed us two daily papers. There had been violent religious clashes in the town and martial law was still in operation. In the *Pakistan Times* and the *Civil and Military Gazette*, two gentlemen, both clearly in bad faith, were attacking France, saying that her "sordid colonial policy is a violation of all human liberties". One of them, describing himself as the head of the Department of History in Lahore University, began his article: "Do you know why France wishes to keep Indo-China? It is because all her factories would be compelled to close down if she lost Indo-Chinese raw materials."

Aliette's meal over, I hurried back to the Airways' Office. Hurray! The manager, all smiles, informed me that he had got us two free seats. He instantly called up the local press for someone to come and get our story. H'm! I was not at all enamoured of the two Communist rags I had just seen.

A reporter arrived on a motor-cycle in a thunder of open exhaust.

"What are your paper's political views?" Aliette asked.

"Oh—well—we're in opposition. . . ."

"What sort of opposition?" she insisted.

"Why—we're a bit on the Left. . . ."

"You mean you're Communists?"

"Oh! you know . . ."

"Come! A photograph, ladies and gentlemen!"

He brought out his camera but, "Oh! No!" my wife cried. "I won't be photographed for a Communist paper!"

The journalist and the airways manager stared at us; things looked as though they might take an ugly turn. Fortunately at this moment a queer series of explosions and puffing noises filled the avenue and a most peculiar vehicle came in sight. On the bonnet was a placard: "London—Sydney—London." A big, bearded man was driving it. I signed to him and he stopped; a blue-eyed young woman jumped out. They saved the situation; the photographer and his camera were instantly all over them.

"Hullo."

"Hullo."

"Where are you off to?"

"Paris. And you?"

The man roared with laughter; his charming wife contemplated us fondly.

"To London! Hohoho!"

The car was an old taxi. It had already been across Australia and Asia. On the roof was a mass of lumber, petrol-tins, and such.

"Yes," sighed the young woman sadly. "We're going home now."

"But since you're English, how will you get through Iran?"

"Hohoho!"

His burst of laughter was so infectious that we all laughed and so did the crowd that had collected round us.

"Why! If we can't get through Iran we'll go round by Russia, eh, Nora?"

Nora, meanwhile, had got a small spirit lamp out of a box and was heating some water. Ten minutes later, still watched by the crowd, we were enjoying a delicious cup of tea.

"Well——"

"Well——"

"Good-bye. Perhaps we shall meet again on the road."

"Perhaps we will. Anyway, if you're going through Paris mind you look us up. We'll manage somehow." I gave this charming soul my card.

"Thanks. So long. Have a good time."

"So long."

They climbed back into their old London cab, which again filled the street with noise, and set off on further adventures. We caught sight of their car one night before leaving Kabul. Then they vanished. We wondered, sometimes, what became of them. Did they get through Persia? Or Russia? Or did their taxi fall to pieces in their hands?

Some weeks after we got back to Paris we found the ancient taxi parked outside the house we live in. "What a coincidence!" Aliette cried. "It must be our friends from Lahore!"

The concierge emerged from his lair.

"Oh! Monsieur Lapierre! I didn't know what to do. Two English people came, and they looked so strange I sent them up the back way."

At this we laughed a lot. We found our friends clinging to the back-door bell.

"Hullo-ullo-ullo . . ."

We spent a delightful week taking them around. The poor dears had not a ha'penny. But they had brought back a superb set of photographs which they hoped to sell to some illustrated paper. They had tried three in vain when the *Auto-Journal* made an offer both for the photographs and a story, so our friends went back to London richer than they had ever been.

Lahore is a clean, tidy, almost pretty town. The manager of the Airways had taken quite a liking to us and invited us to visit some of the monuments. At the chief mosque I was not allowed in, wearing shorts, and had to bribe an old man to lend me a piece of linen to tie round my waist. We even managed to climb to the top of a minaret and enjoy a wonderful view of the city. It looked like a big oasis in that dry and thirsty land.

In the evening we went to the cinema. The hall was strictly divided, men on one side, women on the other. Only one row was reserved for couples. The women were mostly veiled and remained so throughout the entertainment. Beside us sat a huge, broad-shouldered male and a tiny woman, her face and body entirely hidden in her pale pink veil. At the end we were asked to stand in honour of the Pakistan flag, which appeared on the screen accompanied by loudspeakers singing the Pakistan national anthem.

37

Through Afghanistan

By air from Lahore to Peshawar, by road to Kabul, then on to Persia. At Peshawar, by great good luck, a friendly compatriot whom we met on the plane, Desplanques, the agent for Michelin in these parts, offered to take us in his company's car over the famous Khyber Pass to the Afghanistan capital. Also two Italians whose transport had failed them. So there were five of us besides the driver, not to mention the luggage and an ice-box containing the Italians' cargo of German beer, ham, sardines, etc. "Bit of a squeeze," said Desplanques, "but the heavier we are the less we'll bump over the awful roads."

From Peshawar onwards the mountains were all about us and everywhere we saw the men of the mountains, the Afghans with their pink cheeks and fur caps. No more of the thin, weedy, weakly types of the Peninsula. And no more of the great heat. In May the land was just emerging from winter; the mountain-tops were snowy, the glaciers scarcely melting.

The road at first was narrow but tarred; we zigzagged in moderate safety along the edge of precipices, below hills bristling with guns, above valleys thick with anti-tank devices. Paths had been cut out of the rock, and up them trailed long processions of camels on their way to the higher plateaux. Women, close-wrapped in black veils, swayed their bodies rhythmically in time with their mounts' slow swaying.

But at a clump of trees and beside a noisy mountain-stream, where stands the barrier that is the actual Afghanistan frontier, the asphalt stopped and the road became no more than a rough track full of big stones. Our driver was of an impetuous disposition. We drove at breakneck speed, jumping, it seemed, from boulder to boulder. We skirted ravines, missing them by a hairs-

187

breadth. A huge lorry descended upon us full tilt. Aliette clenched her teeth, I shut my eyes. We got by to the sound of scraping metal. We bounced, we hit our heads on the roof, we clung desperately to our seats; the Italians emitted sinister, hiccuping noises. At times, by the roadside, we noticed cairns surmounted by white banners, the tombs of priests, saintly Muslims. It is mostly in such places that the nomads pitch their big, dark tents, hang up their lanterns and sleep while the camels browse among the stones. Thieves and murderers will do no harm here; they believe that if they did the holy men would rise from their graves to punish them.

At nightfall we stopped before a little stone house. This, it appeared, was the hotel where we were to dine and sleep. Dead beat after our exhausting run, we entered. Not a soul was to be seen. One of the Italians, his face and beard white with dust, hunted through room after room and at last discovered a youth fast asleep on a pallet. He dragged him along, and we made signs inquiring if we could have some rice cooked for us and glasses to drink out of. We followed the lad into the kitchen, which was in an indescribable state of confusion. Collecting up some tumblers, he plunged them into a basin of dirty water, pulled out of a cupboard a sheet that was nearer black than white and prepared to wipe the tumblers. At this the Italian leapt upon him, livid with rage, wrenched the filthy cloth out of the lad's hands and cursed him in as many languages as he could lay tongue to. His companion (no beard, only a moustache à la Groucho Marx) roared with laughter. "But my dear fellow! We are in Afghanistan!"

The boy, dumbfounded, dropped the glasses.

After a copious meal, liberally washed down with Munich beer, our two friends, more than a little tight, started to tell spicy Italian stories. The Mediterranean and its rich humour were with us, and in our little inn, lost on the high Afghan plateau, we spent some of the most hilarious hours of our tour. Our experience with the bedrooms was not so funny. A scream of disgust: the bearded Italian had discovered that the sheets on his bed had clearly been the background of an orgy. A scream of fear: Aliette had butted into a goat. The creature's unhappy bleating sent us all into fits of laughter.

A deliciously cool night; we had not slept like this for months.

Aliette, who is usually slow to get up, was ready before I was.

And off we went again along the infernal road. In one village that was but a single street men were sitting before small cafés drinking tea to the strains of much noisy music. Samovars lingered on the tables. We stopped to buy some ice in the hope of keeping our last bottles of beer cool. A great lump of hardened snow was brought to us. It seems they can keep it so, buried underground, for months. At other places we passed huge caravanserais, their battlemented, ochre walls glowing almost red in the sunshine. Through the iron gates one could see herds of donkeys, trains of camels, being loaded for the next stage of their journeys. Goats strayed among the rocks, watched over by long-haired dogs. In the distance the river was hidden in the greenest greenery, and presently we too found trees on either side of the road and a big oasis. In the fields soldiers were manœuvring. I should say that, after Peshawar, while the road itself was safe enough, if you had left it by a yard the guns would have gone off by themselves. The men we saw were armed to the teeth—rifles, daggers, revolvers— their chests laden with cartridges. The smart thing is to look as warlike as possible. You are fond of your weapon and polish it as though it were your most precious toy. In the oasis were regular troops and officers, big men wearing swords and German peaked caps. The white hills towered above them.

A few houses encircled by *pisé* walls; a tramcar overturned beside two tramlines that go nowhere; women, thickly veiled, on bicycles; wide crossroads and a policeman solemnly presiding from a wooden platform over non-existent traffic; a jeep tearing by in its cloud of dust; the slow, undulating gait of camels— Behold! the threshold of Afghanistan's capital. It was the most backward spot that we had seen so far, but the air was fresh and pure and the mountains lent the scene an extraordinary grandeur.

For a hundred yards or so the road became as smooth as velvet; Kabul has just that much asphalt. Big men trotted by on their little horses, in and out of the tangled stream of carts and bicycles that flowed between an ancient, tumble-down picture palace and a leprous, yellow-painted building picked out in white, calling itself the Grand Hotel of Kabul. The Italians, hitherto silent in their contemplation of the landscape, burst out violently: "No! That is too much!"

Yet this was the hostelry where all visiting foreigners must lodge. We entered. An exceptionally dirty man, his face unshaven for three days at least, was asleep behind the counter. The bearded Italian gave him a shake.

"Hi, you! Are you going to wake up?"

The man opened one eye and considered his interlocutor with deep attention.

"Where are the rooms reserved for Mr Papanoni and Mr Romani?"

The man shut his eye.

Behind him hung a washed-out poster: "Come to Italy for the Holy Year." Outside, the veiled women continued to pass on their bicycles, ghostly figures; the noise of a few motor-hooters was sporadically deafening; on the shelf of a grocer's shop, cheek by jowl, lay a packet of Lucky Strikes and a box of Soviet matches.

We left the Italians and the hotel manager to their battle. Aliette's check shirt and black jeans attracted a lot of notice from the passers-by, especially the mysterious, ghostly ladies whose feet, we were surprised to see, were often shod in high-heeled shoes. A gust of wind lifted a veil and, to my wife's still greater amazement, there was a glimpse of a neat, black suiting.

Our friend Desplanques took us to the house of a French professor and his wife who most charmingly invited us to stay with them. For the first time for many months we were able to enjoy a true home atmosphere. Our hostess performed touching acts of kindness and ingenuity to make our visit comfortable. Her husband taught physics at the French lycée. Among his pupils were the king's three sons, fine young men, he said, with already cultured minds. It seems that although girl students have no future in their own country and women, under the new régime, are still more or less where they were, the boys are making great progress. One graduate from Kabul passed first in higher mathematics at Montpellier, and the Afghan philosophy class is quite up to the level of any French provincial lycée. There is also a French school of medicine; the one doctor who, twenty-five years ago, sought to heal wounds by applying a verse of the Koran to the affected part, has been replaced. Islam forbids dissection, but hospitals are being built and there is a six years' course for medical students. The young Afghans are very keen on sport; they bicycle and play hockey and football with zeal. But I was most interested, of course, to know of the lycées and the medical school that have done so much to link Afghan hearts to France.

But having reached Kabul we had to find a means of leaving it. The usual way for foreigners is by that Peshawar road which had brought us here, and then by air to Karachi where the Air France planes touch down almost every day *en route* for Europe. For several reasons, we did not wish to go that way. The first being that, on principle, we would retrace our steps; the second that we wanted to see Persia; the third that we certainly could not afford the international airlines; and the last that our idea was not to hold the record for travelling round the world without money but to learn as much as we could of strange lands by getting to know the natives.

We were told that a small company, suggestively named the Himalayan Airline, carries goods and a few passengers from Bombay to Karachi, to Zahidan in south Persia and to Kabul. So, one fine morning, we called on the company's agent, a tall, slim Indian named Roy Chowdree. He was young and elegant and refined, spoke choice English and bore himself like a prince. He admitted at once that he had fallen a victim to Aliette's charm, and instantly granted us two tickets for Zahidan, a little town in the Iranian desert from which, he assured us, we could easily get to Teheran. Quite ideal!

We strolled in the bazaar where I lost Aliette. An hour later I found her deep in argument with a carpet merchant. He had unrolled all his marvellous stock, but unfortunately even the smallest, even the little mats you put on camels, were much too dear. The Kabul carpet men have agreed among themselves to keep prices up, and we had to abandon all thoughts of purchase.

38

Lost in the Desert

AT DAWN we closed our bags and went to the offices of the Himalayan Airline. Empty! Everything closed! An attendant signed to us that the plane had gone. Disaster . . . I jumped on to the man's bicycle and rode full speed to the high white wall where a gilded shield proclaimed: *République Française. Ambassade de France.* I pushed open the big wooden door and rang peal after peal on the porter's bell. The man came out, half asleep, a gun in his hand.

"Quick! Quick! Bring out a car and take us to the aerodrome!" Desperately I waved my arms trying to make my full meaning clear. While he got ready I rushed back to Aliette, who was waiting for me in the street, surrounded by our luggage. She waved to me to stop at once, but I could not: the bicycle had no brakes. A car was standing by her. What *is* happening? I jumped off and ran back.

A stout, somewhat agitated-looking gentleman got out of the car. The chauffeur started the motor racing.

"Hurry up!" Aliette hissed in my ear. "It's the Prime Minister himself. He is going by the same plane and will take us to the aerodrome."

Oof!

Bowings and scrapings. I offered His Excellency my warmest thanks. He smiled a superior smile, and we were off.

"But where is the aerodrome?" Aliette questioned anxiously.

"It must be that field, by the mountain."

We arrived at a hut crowded with officers in full dress. The motors of the DC 3 were already humming. A five-star general opened the door for us and kissed the Prime Minister's hand. It was almost cold; the wind from the propellers stirred the grasses.

192

In the middle of the airfield was a tomb that compelled the pilots to practise aerobatics of a subtle and crafty sort when taking off or landing. While I saw to the passports I heard my wife inquiring of the great man:

"Why don't they remove the tomb?"

"Because, Madame, in this country a grave is never violated."

Troops presented arms. It appeared that certain representatives of the Government were travelling to London for the Coronation. Much clicking of heels and barking of orders; more and more salaams. A woman in shining black shoes, wrapped in a sort of blue cowl like a phantom, walked up behind her husband. The man was wearing the traditional astrakhan cap; he was a prince on his way with his wife to Europe. They climbed into the plane and occupied the two front seats. We were much intrigued by their mysterious air. A last look at the snowy peaks and we clambered in also, followed by a number of young Afghans in colourful ties. They, apparently, were recruits for the future Afghanistan Air Force, going to India to train. The cabin door slammed to. . . .

Not so very long ago the King of Afghanistan set out for Europe from this aerodrome. He was ill and wanted to be treated in France. It was his wish to travel by the Air France line; he had never been in a plane before. The company sent him a biplane (since no heavy machines could land at Kabul because of the cenotaph), and there was much emotion in the land that fine winter's morning.

The King, fearing to be killed, took with him all the men who might feel disposed to seize his throne. A gorgeously arrayed general weighed the luggage in person on the chance of detecting a time-bomb. In the presence of his entire Court, of the dignitaries of the State, the heads of the Army, the social élite of the kingdom, the Grand Mullah conferred a blessing. The King then stepped into the cabin, bending his head so as not to hit the roof. The crew of the Air France were faced with a difficult proposition. For this reason: in order to give the first royal flight the glamour that the Sovereign's renown demanded, the one and only Afghan fighting squadron had been commandeered as escort. Now the Afghan planes were old, pre-war Junkers. Their pilots frequently lost course and had to come down and ask the shepherds where

N

they were. Also their speed was a third of that of an Air France liner. So the flight had to be planned with extreme care.

The take-off was perfect and the meeting with the escort not too bad. As soon as they were in the air, the plane's captain invited His Majesty to inspect the pilot's cockpit. The hostess saw to the comfort of the remaining dignitaries. Presently a series of deep air-pockets shook the plane in a most disquieting manner, and the hostess had to snatch up the luncheons of the alarmed passengers. What had happened, they wondered, in there with the vanished King? However, they touched down safely at Kandahar, and the escort managed, if with some difficulty, to join them. A grand procession filed across the desert. The security men saw to it meanwhile that the pilots did not play cards "which might have made them nervous". At Herat, the next stop, everyone was presented, amidst scenes of great pomp, with a superb Afghan carpet, a sumptuous gift from His Majesty. The escort returned to base and the Air France liner bore its precious cargo on to Teheran. Crossing the Persian frontier, the Iranian Ambassador to Kabul rose, removed his belt and bowing to the King said: "I have the honour to receive your Majesty in my country."

A few hours later the plane was over the Mediterranean. As they reached France the pilot threw open the door of the cockpit and cried, "Your Majesty! Your Majesty! You are in France!"

The King got to his feet with great dignity, took off his gold watch, hit it a smart knock on the back of his seat to stop it and handed it to the pilot with the single word "Thanks".

The long grasses flattened; we were off. From where we sat we could see, right in front, the top of a finely curled head—the intriguing lady. The plane bounced about on the uneven ground; on either side the high-tension pylons were pointing to the sky. The lady shifted in her seat, half rose. Hop! We left the ground behind and swooped forward in the direction of a forbidding mountain chain, wreathed in small white clouds which our wings just grazed. The crew could have no idea of the weather conditions; there was not a meteorological station within a thousand miles, which is why the Kabul run is considered dangerous and is only flown by one plane a week. After the mountains we passed over a limitless desert, scored here and there by jagged points of rock. The shadow of our plane glided over the golden sand in the grand spring sunshine. A group of beaten-earth houses appeared beside a runway that seemed to stretch, straight and flat, to the softly milky horizon. On it a detachment of soldiery was drawn up. This was Kandahar. We glided down and landed and a tall officer in riding-breeches, his sword clanking on his leg, stepped forward to salute and welcome the visiting VIPs. They descended, one by one—all, alas! but the strange lady whose face we had not seen. Guttural shouts, the band playing the Afghan national anthem. The sky was dark blue, the soil a rich ochre, the air pure. The wings of the plane glittered; it was a fine sight. The soldiers tramped past, preceded by the odd music of the "March of the Camels in the Desert", and vanished into the endless sands.

The music died away, became no more than a dim murmur. Big men in turbans brought up tins of petrol and filled the tanks in an extremely primitive fashion. We approached a tent in which a positive feast of fruit and cakes was laid out on a big, brightly coloured carpet. From time to time our captain (a tall, thin Indian in a sky-blue uniform) got up and took a sip of petrol to see if it was the right quality. Aliette put away an entire plateful of apricots that an officer had placed before her, much to the amusement of the crew and also of the Prime Minister whose Ramadan fast did not seem to have lasted very long.

Some hours of the same arid, lifeless immensity and we were over Persia. Aliette spent the time at her favourite game, which was to compose crosswords for me to solve. Struggling with them I noticed that to make her task easier she did not hesitate to take the wildest liberties with her spelling. Our ears began to buzz, we were losing height; houses came into view; it was Zahidan. On our left a magnificent white cement runway disappeared into the distance, apparently empty. The landing was infinitely pleasanter than in the Afghan desert. An armed sentinel rushed to the cabin door. He was a pitiful spectacle with his badly shaven face, his too-short trousers, his down-at-heel shoes and his pale, yellow-braided linen uniform that reminded one of a circus attendant.

Wonder of wonders! The mysterious lady emerged, and, behold! a white silk shirt, a grey suit, silk stockings, a crocodile handbag, a cigarette, diamonds, and crimson finger-nails! We gaped in astonishment.

N*

A large and dirty man in a great hurry brought us a Customs form and an adorable little gang of Sikh boys chased each other, shouting, round the plane. The lady produced a golden flapjack, looked at herself in the glass, touched her hair, made up her lips and went for a walk. A turbaned gentleman with a rolled beard, wearing a tweed coat that, Aliette said, was beautifuly cut, came up to us and said in good English:

"Garbandah Singh. I am the Company's agent. Please tell me in what way I can be of service to you."

We thanked him and asked our usual question: "How can we get to Teheran as quickly as possible?"

"The next plane is on Saturday, that is in five days. There are motor-coaches but they take several days to reach the capital. And you may not cross Iran without a special permit from the police, which you can only get in Teheran. So you will be obliged to wait for Saturday's plane."

We looked at each other in consternation. A few hundred yards away was a cluster of the usual mud houses.

"Is that Zahidan?"

The Sikh nodded.

"Charming!" said Aliette. "Lots of fun! Five days in this wilderness."

The VIPs in the astrakhan caps, the now unveiled lady, her long reddened cigarette-end crushed out, the twelve ferocious future aces of the Afghan Air Force, the nice Indian crew, had climbed back into the plane and were off down the runway, *en route* for Bombay.

So we were left alone in the splendid but inhuman emptiness. The very houses were so low that they seemed part of the sand. The Company's agent deposited us before a narrow wooden door on which was written in Arabic characters: The Inn of Zahidan.

We knocked and a very large lady opened the door. She could hardly walk she was so fat. She rested her large arms on her belly and greeted us in the few words of French she knew: "Good-day, sir. Welcome. I am Greek."

Carrying our luggage we followed her down a narrow passage that stank most abominably (the cesspool was surely near by) into a sort of patio. Tables were set in a semi-circle about a well; on the left an old woman was busy with an oven that smelt strongly of frying; on the right a door stood open on to a little white-walled room containing two beds. Our room. It seemed clean.

But Aliette had to wash. That was of first importance.

How? Our landlady vanished and returned with an enormous basin and a bucket of water. We had still not finished our ablutions when the old woman burst in and gave us to understand, by signs, that someone was asking for us. I got my clothes on and followed her.

A man in a white linen suit and topee came forward and said in a thin little voice:

"Mister Lapierre? I am Mister Deo, the Indian Vice-Consul." Smiling, he expressed the habitual formula of greeting and added: "Zahidan is not very comfortable or very amusing but I should like to make your visit as pleasant as possible. If you care for tennis we would be happy to receive you in our club."

Club! he had said. Club!

I made him repeat it. A club in this desert? Life was really wonderful. Our shipwreck in the sands looked like turning into a delightful holiday.

Actually the club was nothing like a club—a whitewashed *pisé* shanty.

No matter. At tea-time we went there and found our Sikh surrounded by a lot of other Sikhs in bright turbans. The Brahmin Vice-Consul was also present with his plump young Jain assistant and the assistant's wife, who looked charming in a pale green sari and was nursing a baby of exquisitely imperturbable serenity. A servant brought us shoes and rackets and we started on a closely contested match. Aliette shrieked every time she missed the ball, sending the onlookers into fits of laughter.

"You can't play for nuts," she shouted at me between two disastrous backhanders.

"What about you? I thought you were always at the Racing Club?"

"I've forgotten all I knew——" And hup! the ball soared over the boundary.

After that we drank tea and listened to soft music. I turned a knob on the wireless set and out came a shrill woman's voice: "This is Paris. Here is the news." In a corner of the terrace four men were playing bridge.

Rich Indian merchants also frequented the "club". Apart from business they did not mix much with the locals. Heirs of the best British traditions, they made these daub walls "highly exclusive".

The Zahidan water is not fit to drink. As it would have been tiresome to absorb tea all day long it occurred to us one morning to boil a saucepan of water and add some chlorine. With more than doubtful-looking swabs, we rinsed out some old beer bottles and filled them, our hostess having dipped her black finger into the saucepan to see if the water was cool enough. The results of this delicate operation were of course quite impossible. We put our trust in God and quenched our thirst with the *aqua simplex* from the well, which was open to the sky and constantly received this or that scrap of rubbish.

For our meals we were content with vast platefuls of rice, occasionally flavoured with a little chicken. The Vice-Consul had warned us categorically against eating any other meat. It was not for fear of germs; you had only to take one look at the native butcher's stall.

On our second evening the head of the Zahidan District Police asked us to dinner. Round about eight o'clock of an exquisitely starry night, a chauffeur fetched us in a jeep. We drove through a labyrinth of dark alleys to a high mud wall and a porch, under which we passed into a big garden. We stopped before a low white bungalow, and a number of people sitting in basket chairs rose at our approach. It was difficult at first, in the dusk and the confusion, to make out which were our hosts. A shy little man with a bald head, wearing a blue, red-braided uniform, shook us by the hand vigorously, and half in French, half in English, introduced his wife, an imposing matron in black taffeta, gloved to the elbow and heavily made up; then his daughter, whose red dress was cut extremely low, her heels very high, her hair done in a crown on top of her head and her cheek, as a supreme touch of elegance, adorned with a beauty spot; finally his son, rather the Paris spiv with his thick crêpe-soled shoes and narrow tie. Then there were the guests: the Colonel of the Military Police, typically German-looking in a cream uniform; his wife in a skin-tight silk frock, her shoulders draped in a mantilla and her fingers ringed with sham diamonds; the local midwife, crimson-lipped, aggressively red-haired, also wearing long gloves; and a spotty youth with plastered hair who was Judge of the Civil Courts.

They all sat down and looked at each other as before. Large glasses of pink lemonade were being handed round; we had to exercise prodigious cunning to avoid drinking more than a little of it.

"You are pleased with Zahidan?" the military judge asked us, and instantly burst out laughing.

"Of course!" we replied in chorus.

"Oh no," said the young Judge in stumbling French. "Zahidan —Zahidan—Bastille of Iran! You agree?"

Roars of laughter. The Colonel, fiddling with his glass, echoed as though to himself: "Yes. Zahidan, Bastille of Iran. . . ."

His son wound up a gramophone and, grating and squeaking, we heard the sickly sweet voice of Tino Rossi. Everyone joined in the song.

Aliette glanced at me. She was amazed—the huge desert, the wonderful night, and these men, these women in their rustling dresses, that howling voice from the half-cracked record. . . . It was really very odd.

Presently we got up and went into the garden where multitudes of drinks were set out on a big table; beer and spirits and the delicious Persian sweet wines. The Colonel filled and refilled the glasses and toast succeeded toast very rapidly amidst more roars of laughter.

"Death to England!" cried one.

"Long live France!" cried another.

"Death to Zahidan!"

"Long live Moussadeq!"

"Long live Tino Rossi!"

The excitement increased. The gramophone shrieked louder. The military judge clung to the midwife's arm and stroked her hair; the civil Judge swung Aliette off into a wild dance. Everyone began to dance; I found myself drawn into the arms of the young lady with the beauty spot and glued to her in a passionate embrace. The noise was terrific. We jigged from one foot to the other, snatched violently at a different partner, spun her about, snatched at her again and hopped some more. The company then collapsed breathless into chairs and rested a while. The midwife was mopping her cheeks with a lace handkerchief. Our hostess went up to her and whispered in her ear, whereupon she rose and hurried away; she was wanted for a difficult confinement. The party continued. Its next stage took us to a table spread with food: wings of chicken, kabobs of mutton, meat patties, rice, vegetables, a feast to which Aliette and I, in defiance of all proper caution, did considerable honour. My wife cannot stand two drops of alcohol. Flushed, her cheeks dimpled, she gave me large seductive smiles. The festivities went on far into the lovely night.

Our adieux were most touching. We swore that we would return some day to Zahidan. The good Colonel, half-drunk, slapped me on the shoulder and muttered affectionately that he loved France. He broke into the refrain of the Marseillaise. Salaams were endless. The women peeled off their gloves, and their hands floated up to my lips. Conscientiously I did my duty all round. The jeep brought us back to our inn, which was locked and barricaded so that we had to hammer at it for a long while before our old Greek landlady came out in her nightgown to let us in. By the door a man in rags lay sleeping.

The long wait came to an end. On the day before we left, the Teheran–Bombay plane, which was to pick us up on its return journey, brought in a charming young Afghan couple and their baby. They were returning from Paris where the man had just taken his degree in forensic medicine. The first in Afghanistan! He was tall and black-haired; she was young and pretty and fair-skinned. In a couple of days she would be wearing the veil.

We had almost emptied our pockets, but our fares were paid and now we were squatting in a little tent beside the runway waiting for the plane. Outside, the soldiers' bayonets glittered; it was very hot. A tiny hum sounded in my head, so low I felt that it might be imaginary. A black dot appeared in the blue sky. It crossed the mountain chain that closes the horizon, grew bigger, swerved, dropped, turned; its shadow hovered over the sand. It was the one and only plane of the Iranian Airways, the company that used to be so rich in accidents that it was nicknamed the Inshallah Airways.

One passenger stepped out. He was a dreadful old man with a bandaged head, all bent and so grossly stout that he could scarcely get through the door; he stood there and passed water in front of everybody before getting back into the plane. The crew was international: the captain is French, the co-pilot German, the wireless operator Irish, the steward Persian, and the hostess Greek.

Not very long after we left the salt desert behind we saw, out of the porthole, a great green mass: Teheran.

39

At Teheran

SATURDAY—a bad day to arrive in an unknown place. ... The company's coach took us into the centre of the city. Wide avenues again and houses scrawled over with the slogan: "Yankee Go Home!" After our trek to Kabul, our week in the desert, Teheran seemed the very acme of civilisation.

A big building: Air France. We were set down, our minds concerned only with one thought: where should we sleep that night? Anyway, we decided to try it; they might be able to help.

"Most certainly," the foreman of the landing-ground answered. "I can give you the address of the boarding-house where my crews always stay." He added with a grin: "It's very cheap."

It should be said that our cash account was almost at death's door. A tall and amiable gentleman, however, walked into the office and we were introduced. He was the Air France agent.

"I suggest you go over the way," he said. "Behind that old house opposite there is the Teheran Club. I am a member. I'll write you a chit and perhaps they'll give you a guest room. If that doesn't work, don't fret, we'll think up something else."

Our thanks were indeed heartfelt. And no sooner said than done. The nice young secretary of the Club, Irene Mikeladze, received us and led us at once to a huge room. The gods were with us, and we ran back to thank the Air France manager again.

"Wait a minute," he said. "Whom do you know in Teheran?"

"No one!"

"Right ..." He hesitated for a moment, then: "Listen. You must meet the director of the museum. And M. and Mme C.... too; they're working on ancient Persian manuscripts, and ..." Ten minutes later, in the simplest and most straightforward manner, we found ourselves invited to dinner with a whole bunch of fascinating scientific people.

So our time in Teheran was quite delightful. At the club, which was a real club this time, we made a number of acquaintances: Persians, Italians, Lebanese, French. Each one was more pleasant than the other and we lived almost entirely apart from the prevailing Persian disquiet. This was, nevertheless, the first Police State of our journey, and we spent long days at the Prefecture getting papers that would allow us to prolong our stay and to go to Ispahan. We were asked for two photographs, then for four; at one moment we were refused any kind of permit and threatened with expulsion; the next we were treated like honoured guests. Everything was completely inconsequential.

Once, walking down the Firdausi Avenue, a little girl in pigtails, wearing the uniform of a religious school, sidled up to us, muttered a few words and hurried on her way. It took us quite a few moments to realise that what the demure and angelic-looking infant had actually whispered in her appalling English was, "Yankee go home!" We were so astonished that we burst out laughing.

Back at the club we spoke of our encounter to an American colonel, a police counsellor. "I'm not surprised," he commented, waving his glass of vodka. "I used to find my house scribbled all over with the same thing. I got so annoyed removing the marks that I had a large copper plate put up, clearly engraved: 'Yankee go home!' I set it on the door. Since then my walls have stayed clean."

The newspapers announced that André Malraux was in Iran. Next day a French friend told us the following story:

The scene was the billiards room of the Teheran Club; the actors a Canadian, an American, and our friend.

Said the American to the Frenchman: "You know the young couple who are going round the world?"

"Yes."

"How is it they went to China?"

"To China?"

"Yes. Didn't you know? They're passionate Communists. They stayed a long time in China."

"That's so," the Canadian put in. "They've even written books about Communism. They're bad lots."

"Well, if it's like that . . ."

"You see," he went on to us. "I didn't know if you had expressed extreme opinions or not so I couldn't defend you properly. And then it suddenly dawned on me and I told Bob he was an idiot. 'You're muddling them up with the writer Malraux who used to be a Communist and has written books about China.'"

The American saw he had made a mistake and went back serenely to his game of billiards. There are countries where a remark of that sort would be quite enough to get a foreigner expelled on the spot.

We had several long talks with a young Iranian student. He spoke of the youth of his country and everything he said revealed a deep distress.

"What can you expect? We have had no time to adapt ourselves to the new conditions. What took Europe a century and a half we have had to do in twenty-five years. That is why we are so disturbed. Everything is vague and floating. The political situation is to blame. One day we are put in prison for 'subversive activities'. Next day we are let out, we don't know why. One morning an allowance is suppressed. By evening our registration fees at the Faculty are put up. . . . And we know, anyway, that we've no future. The country needs constitutional foundations that would be solid and unchanging. Instead of that it's all fog and no one knows what tomorrow will be like. Moussadeq gave us hope, but he is not behaving as we expected. We were all for him when he nationalised the oil. Yet that has been a failure."

"But why?" interruped Aliette. "Why are only ten per cent of the students studying engineering? Why don't they try to take over now that the English have gone? It's a perfect opportunity."

The young man wiped his glasses. He was very shortsighted and they were very thick.

"The English," he continued calmly, "recruited a few Iranian students and trained them in their school at Abadan. They chose them themselves. Not many. They were sent on afterwards to Birmingham. They had to undertake to work for the English and it is from this imperialistic treatment that we have suffered so much. Those of our men who worked for the English had advantages the others couldn't have. There is no engineer's degree or diploma in Iran today. If most of us take up Law or Literature it is because they allow us to earn a living while we are students. Science or medicine wouldn't leave us any spare time."

"And yet," I pointed out, "a lot of Persians study abroad? Some of them are given scholarships?"

"Yes, of course, but nine times out of ten they never come back. They prefer to try their luck elsewhere. And they're quite right."

"And so?"

"And so young people here are exasperated and turn towards Communism. Iran got tired of the English and the Russians and looked to the Third Force. That was at the time we were all crazy about jazz and American films. But America took England's side and our dream of the Third Force collapsed. No, there is no future, there are no opportunities. The schools only train you to be bureaucrats, never to develop any personal initiative. So most of the young people who are atheists are attracted to Marxism. Atheism is the first step in their evolution. That is not new, of course. Persian poetry has always cried out against an imaginative and fantastic view of life. Don't you remember the poem that begins: 'Oh, Lord God. In truth all wrong-doing has been brought into the world by you'? Our young people today want to be free of Islam. But this freedom can't come from the State, nor from their families. A father behaves like a tyrant. He has no respect for his wife, and the sons are beginning to feel indignant at the way their mothers and sisters are bullied in the name of old traditions and superstitions in which they, as atheists, no longer believe. Which means division in the home and a leaning towards revolution. In Iran, Communism is the only defender of equality between men and women. Its most fervent followers are young intellectuals who want social action. For the first time boys and girls have come together and evolved a programme that is common to them both. On Thursday evenings more than five hundred of them go out in 'peace caravans' as they are called and travel about the country. They visit the peasants and sing to them and discuss social problems so as to stir their minds and make them understand that they have rights."

"What do the professors say to that?" asked Aliette.

"Nothing. At least they don't express an opinion. Most of them, if they want to earn even a bare living, have to do extra work outside their classrooms. They avoid talking politics in school."

"What sort of men are they?"

"Oh! men without ambition. Or men who have gifts but no means of exploiting them."

He paused for a long time and then said, very slowly, looking straight into our eyes: "I must seem terribly pessimistic to you. But all this is only too true. If the situation doesn't clear up quickly, Persia will go the way China has gone. She has her own characteristic symbolism and her own metaphysics and is creating an Oriental Marxism. Her Communists are inspired rather by China than by Russia. To put matters at their least bad, one can say that in its new awakening the youth of Iran is faced with a dilemma; to look to the West that can bring, among other things, liberty but has left such unhappy memories, or to look East to China that seems to offer such a wonderful example."

At last we were given our permits to visit Ispahan, the city that Malraux sets beside Florence and Venice as the most beautiful in the world. There was unfortunately only one means of travelling the two hundred and fifty miles that separated us from Ispahan, namely the motor-coach. And still more unfortunately, the only seats available were at the back, just over the wheels. The road started off all right but soon became shattering, and we had to cling on as we had already done in Afghanistan so as not to smash our heads against the roof. Since tar is an oil product it seems absurd that Persian roads should be so bad! At this rate cars could not last very long. It was not surprising to learn that Iran had imported twenty million *tomans*' worth of foreign makes last year and thirty millions' worth of spare parts.

We stopped at a little village inn for luncheon. The people thought we were Americans.

"So you enjoyed the journey?" a man asked us with exquisite irony. "The roads aren't so good as in the States, eh?"

His companions looked at him and laughed.

Aliette jumped to her feet, and, giving him a hard stare, said drily: "We're French."

The man blushed, stammered and departed, downcast, to join his friends, who seemed disconcerted too. French or American, the inn-keeper fleeced us well and thoroughly.

An interminable field of opium poppies, their heads swaying softly in the light breeze; a prolonged examination of our papers, and we entered the ancient capital of Persia. Only a vague memory remained of its past greatness. In the days of the Parthians and the Sassanids it was a famous artistic and commercial centre; later, in the seventh century, the Muslims took it and then

the Seljuks, who made it the capital of Persia. In the fourteenth
century it was invaded by the Moghuls and did not recover its
place till the sixteenth century under Shah Abbas, the great king
of the Safavi dynasty. The town's chief monuments date from this
last period. At the beginning of the eighteenth century the
Afghans seized it but lost it again; from then on it has steadily
declined so that today one of the "glories of the world" has
scarcely two hundred thousand inhabitants.

The motor-coach drove up a well-treed avenue and deposited
us in the courtyard of an hotel.

Instructive and salutary. We journey from one mosque to
another, from palaces to Armenian churches, from the souks to the
waters of the Zayandehrood, wandering at our leisure through
this peaceful place of fruit and flowers. The Royal Mosque seemed
to us the most beautiful. At the end of the sixteenth century Shah
Abbas designed a great square which he proposed to make the
loveliest imaginable. Water ran all about it; at its centre was the
polo ground. We had not known that polo was originally a Persian
game and had supposed that the miniatures and engravings we
had been shown represented hunting scenes.

Shah Abbas then built the palace of Ali Quaper and immediately opposite, to balance it, the Mosque of Lutfallah, and
finally, on the west of the square, the celebrated Royal Mosque
that everyone agrees is the most magnificent of all Persian buildings.

Before entering one goes through a porch flanked by two
minarets inset with blue mosaics of incredibly delicate design.
Over the door, the lintel was encrusted with a silver pattern that
used to be gilt; on the right the carved stone rim of a little ornamental pool rose above a fine pavement. The central dome was
lined with porcelain tiles; the same tiles of a bright turquoise
colour covered the outer surface; above it was yet another dome,
flanked also by minarets that were even higher than those of the
porch. Inside, at the back of the Mosque, was a throne cut from
a single piece of marble that came from many, many miles away.

But we had to make haste. It was Ramadan and the sanctuary
was full of praying people whose dislike of foreigners was livelier
even than that of the men of Teheran. Aliette, out of respect for
the holy place and so as not to attract attention, had wrapped

herself in a long, dark veil that gave her a most mysterious air.

Between whiles we roamed up and down the bazaar and stood for a long while before the jewellers' stalls. Aliette tried on, one by one, all the astonishing silver bracelets; they were like carved lace. Her eyes as she glanced up from each in turn were bright with desire. But everything was lovely, jewels, miniatures, embroideries.

In the evening at the hotel we sat with a little bald man who had taken a fancy to us and who seemed quite surprisingly cultured. He was an old Grignon student, and had been Iran's Minister of Agriculture; he owned land in Ispahan and spent half his year here, looking after it. His memories of France were extraordinarily sharp and the long monologues in which he expressed his love for our country were very touching.

"You see, my friends," he said, "what is unique about France is that the foreigner at once feels at home there. Iranian students do not like staying in England; they love to be in France. I have travelled in India and also in certain French colonies. The difference is very striking. The English never live side by side with the natives as the French do. I assure you. Wherever they go the English take England with them. It is their clubs do it, their famous clubs. Have you seen the architecture of Bombay? How ridiculous to have built Gothic houses in India! You can't imagine such a thing in Indo-China, can you? Utterly absurd!"

He chuckled to himself before proceeding:

"But what is terrible in France is the endless self-criticism. I was amazed last time I went there at the way everyone cried, 'Oh! but——' In 1939 they said it a hundred times a day. I don't know how often they say it now but possibly three times as often."

"Of course," said Aliette. "But we have so much to blame ourselves for."

"I understand, I understand, but you'd rather talk about Alphonse Daudet than about Donzères-Mondragon. Do you realise how wonderfully gifted France is? I don't know of any country equal to it—not even America. And people forget what France has done in her colonies. Look at Morocco. Think what it would have cost the Government there to make a geological survey and map of the country. But France did it. Do you know that a French technician only costs thirty per cent more in Morocco than he does in Paris? One would have to pay a good man five times more to make him come here. That, my friends, is why we hate England. To enrich herself she has ruined India and Persia and many other countries. She has killed Indian industry. By appropriating our greatest source of wealth she has left us to starve. England always leaves ruin behind her."

A diatribe against the British followed after which the man stopped abruptly, rubbed his moustache and asked in a sharp voice: "Apropos—What is existentialism?"

We sketched out a few vague definitions that seemed to satisfy him.

"I'll tell you why I ask," he said. "Last time I was in France some friends took me to a sort of cave where wild-looking people of both sexes were throwing themselves about to the sound of a peculiarly hysterical kind of music that is called, I believe, jazz. What with the smell of alcohol and sweat and smoke the air in the den was quite unbreathable. After a bit my friend nudged me and said: 'You see that chap over there with the beard and the black shirt flopping over his trousers? That's the new pope of existentialism!' "

The man guffawed loudly. "Tell me," he asked. "Are they mad?"

A long silence came upon us, broken only by the creaking of the cicadas. Slowly and solemnly, his head thrown back, he added, "Look at the sky of Ispahan. I believe it is the most beautiful in the world."

40

End of the Honeymoon Round the World

AND now, back in Teheran, we had to consider our last step, our final departure. Our money was practically exhausted, and after eleven months' wandering the time had come to return to the fold. We were given several opportunities of going to Beyrout by car but we could not wait for them. Our permits had nearly run out and we did not want to end our honeymoon round the world in one of Moussadeq's prisons.

These last days were very happy, relished to the full. Sometimes at night I dreamt that we were back in Paris and then awoke with inexpressible joy to find myself still in the room above the lovely avenue, named Firdausi after the great Persian poet.

We knew very well—we told each other so—that our hearts were torn between apprehension, the anxiety of having to readapt ourselves to a routine life lost and forgotten on the highways of the world, and the delight of seeing France and our families again.

We were still dreaming of adventure. . . .

But the die was cast. By arrangement with Air France, the hour of our going was fixed. It was already Saturday. On Thursday next we should be back in Paris; in four days the honeymoon round the world would be ended. Yet the honeymoon would continue, enriched by memories and a new life.

What a contrast! The difference between the magnificent Constellation that carried us away and the rickety old crates we had known hitherto was almost startling. Our pilot was not a Bangkok man nor a man from Calcutta; he hailed from just outside Paris; and the hostess was not a fat lady in a misty sari but a tall young woman in a navy blue blazer. My mind went back to the take-off at Lahore.

But the pilot was melancholy. "There it is," he sighed. "We're not airmen any more, we're civil servants. The radio is at us every minute, telling us to do this and that. And we must obey. Oh dear! D'you know that when I was on the Rio-Santiago line we had to look for a stretch of grazing with cattle to find out which way the wind was blowing? Cows always feed nose to windward."

The square tower of a mosque rose above a huddle of flat-roofed houses: Damascus. We spent two delightful days in this picturesque town with the French military attaché, taking long walks here and there by its yellow walls and along the road St Paul trod to his conversion. One last glimpse of the Orient and its acrid-smelling souks, its women in coloured veils, its turbaned men and its mosques crowded with pious, mysterious people.

To reach Beyrout, where we had to catch another plane, our only chance was a lift in a car. We got one on the Damascus road where a Buick picked us up and conveyed us to the Lebanese frontier. Another wait, and a stout gentleman in glasses deposited us at the famous ruins of Baalbek.

Perched beneath six tall columns on the topmost of a wonderful flight of steps, we looked down admiringly on the great courtyard and its scattered stones, fragments of pillars, lintels, statues. On our left were the façade and the empty niches of a long building, its roof set with columns. Opposite was the skeleton of what was once a wall. On their side the great stairways descended into the courtyard. The sun was setting, and the building slipped into shadow. Above our heads swallows were wheeling and crying, seeking the broken walls and the colonnade. The hills, far away, were rosy; soft wisps of cloud trailed across the blue sky. But the sun sank lower, and the stones began to lose their pink glow and to turn grey; the swallows pursued their broken, circling flight as the night fell over Lebanon. The muezzin sounded from a minaret; the fast was over. A wasp buzzed; a donkey brayed; a tall poplar bowed before the evening breeze; the stones slept like corpses on a battle-field.

At nightfall we were still on the road. A policeman stopped a car for us, and the driver, a young Lebanese, drove us at top speed round the ravine-bordered curves of his native hills.

But a thousand lights shone on the sea: Beyrout! Good-bye, Asia; this was the Mediterranean! The transition was sudden and shocking. For the first time for many days we were in a town that was all noise and brilliance. The streets were full of American cars; families were seated on the terraces of cafés; the shops were bursting with every sort of goods. No more famine, no more beggary. We had forgotten that there could be a world where folk had fun and an easy life. Aliette, her mouth open like a child before a sweet-shop, stared aghast at a notice hung before a building-site: "Here will be the new Eden Roc."

And in a few hours the sky was clear, the sea blue, the houses white. We were flying to Paris. . . .